FAITH
THROUGH TEARS

Kimberly Richardson

BEYOND
PUBLISHING

New York | Los Angeles | London | Sydney

ISBN Hardcover: 978-1-637922-52-1

DEDICATION

I dedicate this book to our Heavenly Father and my mom, Barbara Jean Richardson. God, You have always heard my praises and cries out to You. All success in life is because of You. You timing has always been perfect, and the lessons have always been necessary. Thank You for walking with me through it all. I continue to feel and see how omnipotent You truly are. Mom, saying I miss you doesn't even begin to express the void in my heart. You will always be my best friend and mentor. Thank you for showing me what true love looks and feels like for myself and others. Because of you, I continue to build upon my relationship with God, and it feels amazing. You've always taught me how to find positives in all situations just by watching you live your life. God and Mom, I see you, I hear you, I feel you, and I thank you.

I want to thank my wonderful children and best friends, Tristen and Ki'en. Your love and support have helped push me to be stronger each day. Your love is of God, and I am so grateful He chose me to be your mom. I pray to make you both proud of me so that you may use my teachings in your lives for days to come. I pray my wisdom from God pours over into you in a way that it will push you through to your next level with God. Always remember that no matter what happens in life, I am proud of you and will always be with you. Never doubt that you were created for a purpose. Ask God to go before you and with you on your day-to-day journey. This life is about being vessels for others. Be that for each other as well. When one is weak, you be the strong one and pick your sibling up in their time of need. Be okay with not always being okay. God will fill in the pieces of your puzzle that needs mending if you allow Him. Never doubt yourself, because I never have and never will. God created you for something very special, and you will achieve that goal that He has for you. I love you both with all that I have. God, I thank You for lending Your children to me. I pray to be everything that You would have me to be for them each and every day. I pray that You continue to cover them with Your wisdom, love, and protection always.

I also want to thank my dad (Willie Joe), sister (De Anna), bothers (Marcus and Justin), nieces (Riley, Ryane, and Grace), nephews (Devin, Micah, and Tucker), our Ingram, Richardson, and extended families, my church family, my 2020-21 Booker T. Washington Elementary School family, my Sorors of the Alpha Kappa Alpha Sorority, Incorporated, my Luminaries family (Transformation Church B-Group), and all my friends.

Dad and Siblings, I cannot begin to say how much I love and appreciate you. We have experienced so much together over the years, and we've always stuck close to each other. That will never change because *"What God has joined together, let no man separate." ~Mark 10:9* Together, we can, and together, we will continue to push through with a purpose. God has equipped us for so much more. Stand strong through all situations. To my entire village, your outpour of love has pushed me to continue to get up and move forward. The saying, "It takes a village," stands true. The way that I have been covered in prayer and the love that has been shown has been nothing but God-fed. God used each one of you to show me that everything will be okay and how loved I truly am. I know that I have a mission to complete, and with God, I will achieve each goal that He has for me. I love you all so much. God has led me to write this devotional journal, and I pray it brings peace, love, and comfort for those in need. *"...with God all things are possible." Matthew 19:26*

CONTRIBUTIONS

Special thanks to de de Cox, my God-fearing friend and Kentucky's best-seller romance author. You have been the best support system throughout my journey of writing this book. You understood that God placed this on my heart and how much it meant to me to finish what I started. I can't thank you enough for your patience and encouragement as I experienced many emotions within each chapter. You have been one of my biggest supporters and cheerleaders throughout the creation of this book, and for that, I thank you from the bottom of my heart. I pray that God continues blessing you in all that you are doing.

Thanks to my publisher, Michael D. Butler with Beyond Publishing Global. Your consistency, hard work, and dedication are greatly appreciated. Thank you for pushing me to publish this gift that God has placed inside of me and allowing me to be open and transparent throughout this journey.

Erica Sharp with Erica Lee Photography has been a part of my little family circle for many years. Erica, thank you for always fitting my little family into your busy schedule and literally capturing a true picture of what my family really means to me. I cherish every photo that you've ever taken and pray they will serve as happy memories for my children for years to come. I love every photo and the memories they hold. It has truly been a blessing to have met you and remained connected throughout the years. May God continue to bless you and your many talents.

TESTIMONIES

"This book shares the story of a daughter who lost not only the woman she called her mom, but her best friend. The author takes you through her journey of this loss. In life, sometimes, we forget it's okay to mourn and even more so, to take the time needed to mourn and heal. This author has shared something more valuable than the words typed or written: she has shared her faith. Knowing that HE can handle everything and finding out that HE truly can and will is the first step to healing. Kim has helped me more than she will ever know."

~de de Cox / Kentucky #1 Romance Author

"When I think grace, poise, and elegance, Kimberly comes to mind. Witnessing her strength and softness as she dealt with the passing of her beloved mother appeared as a testimony to the peace God can provide in the midst of grief. I'm positive that her words, guided by the Holy Spirit and personal life experience, will bring you comfort as well as encourage you through any season of loss. Kind, powerful, and reassuring, this book will remind you that with Our Faithful God by our side, we can surely count it all joy."

~Kannelle Hughes/Head of Sciences Po's East Africa Office, Seasoned Salt of the Earth, Aspiring Luminary

"In part, we Believers acknowledge this divine attribute of God. That is, until the life pains and sorrows hit us so hard that we forget all over again. We forget that God never promised us that the weapons would not form; rather, He said that they would not prosper. We forget that He never promised a life without storms, but He promised to be there with us in the midst. We forget that He said weeping would endure for a night, but joy would meet us in the morning. Ultimately, if we can know and accept that, without a doubt, God loves each and every one of us, then it won't be hard to find the essence of Him as we journey through life and accept all of the terms, conditions, and benefits that come with our salvation! We're in good business with God!

Therefore, when I am having what I like to call "spiritual oversight" of my conditions in my life's journey, I default to Romans 8:28, where it states that ALL things are working together for the good of them who love Him who have been called according to His purpose. That means that even though it looks and feels bad, that my divine terms also come with benefits that make these things shift to serve my ultimate good. However, for most Believers, this is easier said than done. That is why I am so delighted that my Sister in Christ, Kimberly, has been obedient to God's leading in writing this book chronicling her testimony to help both you and me see through life's hardships to seek the positives of God. I know that this book will be a vital resource as we should all seek to be of encouragement one to another as we go through life's ebbs and flows!"

~Tatiana Carter (Daughter of Christ)

PREFACE

~Bible Verse that inspires me and reminds me of mom's teachings~

1 Thessalonians 5:18: Give thanks in all circumstances;
for this is God's will for you in Christ Jesus.

On December 22, 2020, my mom started experiencing lower abdominal pains. The pain was so excruciating that it required my younger brother and dad to put her in a wheelchair to assist with getting her into dad's Jeep. Once she reached the hospital, they admitted her, and within 24 hours, she was taken to Jewish Hospital in Louisville, Kentucky and placed in ICU. There, they discovered she had infection in her bloodstream and lungs, along with a UTI, which caused the pain and confusion that she was experiencing. Throughout her stay at Jewish, she had a combination of good and very tough days, but mom was a fighter through it all! I share more details of "Mom's Fight" at the end of this book.

Fast-forward: On January 10, 2021, at 5:10 a.m., dad called and stated that the hospital contacted him and said that mom had taken a turn for the worse and he needed to get there as soon as possible. My heart rate instantly increased and pounded so hard that I had to concentrate on my breathing. My prayers and emotions went into overdrive. On my bathroom floor, sporadically, my mind allowed the thought of losing my mother, and I literally shook my head trying to erase such thoughts and prayed to God, "Please Lord, heal mom and let the devil know that You are in charge, You are the Healer, and will relieve her from any hurt, harm, or danger that is coming her way." During the wait time, I suddenly got real still and quiet. I no longer could cry or pray. There was a confusing stillness put over my soul. I walked out of my bathroom and sat on my bed in total silence.

At 8:30 a.m., I received a phone call from my dad with the most devastating news that my mom, my best friend had passed away at 8:00 a.m. due to a chain of events. Her little body had experienced Acute Respiratory Failure and Septic Shock. Mom had lived with Sarcoidosis of the liver for many years, which developed into an underlining cause called Nash Cirrhosis. I could not believe what I was hearing. Mom was a fighter and had fought for countless years and always came out on top. She was small and mighty in many ways, but the news was true. Her body was tired, and God was ready to remove her from any additional pain. Even knowing that, my entire body felt a pain that I had never felt in my life. I am not sure what all my dad said after that, because my mind went into total shock. There are no thoughts that I can remember from that moment on, but the feeling is still so clear. My heart pounded so hard that it literally took my breath away. I've never had a heart attack, but at that moment, I felt that I was experiencing something very similar. I couldn't catch my breath, so I had to hold my chest and bend over just to take quick, small breaths. I still have moments of stillness and blurred visions, but I know that I must keep going, because people are counting on me. I also know in my heart that mom is rooting for me as well. My faithfulness to God had to be kicked into overdrive. I pray that I take time out to be refueled by the One that will push me to be greater than the day before.

God will not lead you to a place or into a situation without having a lesson prepared. He is not a pointless God. With Him, every situation will eventually bring consolation. Knowing this, I took time to study His Word. That was the place where I can always find comfort. I began journaling my feelings and the scriptures that spoke to me. During this process, God spoke so clearly by telling me to use what He had already placed inside of me to help heal and be healed. I was being asked to capture my thoughts and transform them into a book to help serve as a healing process for others as well as myself. I knew that was God, because I would never speak about all of these feelings so openly, especially to the world, but I had to remain faithful.

My life felt as it has been turned upside down, and only God could help me put the fragile pieces back together. As I began to create the entries for this book, I used a specific format with headings based on how I heard God speak to me. The topics aren't written in sequential order, because when the emotional triggers occur, there is no order. This helped me realize that there was a purpose in this structure, and that was exactly what I was receiving throughout the chapters of this book. The more I journaled, the clearer I heard God telling me to share my experience with others. Although this has been one of the most difficult things I have even written, I knew that I had to be faithful in His request for my journey of healing spiritually, mentally, emotionally, and physically. I pray this book touches at least one person in a way that God would have it to.

As I completed mom's obituary, I felt as though we were sitting in the same room coming up with the right words to share with all that loved her. With God's help, I spoke these words during her service.

"My Time..."

The Lord told me that it was my time ...

My time to let go of the pain and suffering.

My time to watch over my husband, as he's done for me.

My time to watch our children and grandchildren grow into the wonderful people that God has created them to be.

My time to join my beautiful family of Angels

that have watched over me.

My time to feel honored when meeting our Heavenly Father.

My time to hear, "Well done, My good and faithful servant."

So please don't be sad over my transition; everything will be alright.

I will continue to watch over you

and hope that you feel my presence for days to come.

I will always love each and every one of you as you've loved me.

Sincerely, your wife, mother, grandmother,

sister, auntie, cousin, and friend.

TABLE OF CONTENTS

CHAPTER 1

FINDING POSITIVES
IN ALL SITUATIONS

Bible Verse:

Jeremiah 29:11: For I know the plans I have for you, declares the LORD, plans to prosper you and not to harm you, plans to give you hope and a future.

Why I choose this topic?

Always remember that even in your struggles, there's an inner peace that will eventually come over you. Give yourself grace to receive it. I know where I could be if I didn't train myself to see the positives in all situations. Having the power to seek God in my darkest times always gives me a sense of peace that I want for you as well.

Let's talk:

The enemy will attack you when you are building upon your faith and trust in God. When he can't get to you, he will attempt to attack what you love the most. Be careful not to give the devil your power. Some trials are God's way of showing you that it's your time to step up to your next mission in life. You will not always know the difference in the moment, and that's okay. Speak with God and ask for clarity and guidance as you attempt to move forward in His plans for you.

How do I know this? I've experienced it to its fullest in December and January, when mom was sick. When I spoke with her nurses, I would get positive reports one moment and then reports that were very tough to hear. I was torn between, "Is the devil attacking my mom as a way of showing me that he is stronger than my faith? Or was it God building my family up for our next mission for Him?" I would be on the floor breaking down crying out to God, "Please tell that devil to take his hands off my mom. Allow him to come for me and release her. Please heal her and show him that he has no power over You or our family. I release it all over to You, Lord." There were times I would calm down and have flashes of mom's transition (funeral, me crying, etc.), and I would literally shake my head, trying to erase any negative thoughts. I thought those thoughts were of the devil. I was not losing my faith, but I still felt bad that my mind allowed me to take me there and think those things. I questioned my strength, but never my faith that God was going to "fix" everything, and mom would be okay once again. Although it wasn't in the form that my flesh had hoped for in the moment, He did make everything better for mom, better than I could even imagine.

Always remember that regardless of the many emotions that you may face, God is with you every step of the way. You may question your personal faith, but know that it is okay not to be okay all the time. Lord knows I am not always okay. I continue to have moments of sadness, loneliness, feeling of wanting that separation from others, and disappointment in my ability to be consistent in studying the Word of God. I am thankful that God never gives up on me and finds ways to rebuild those things that I have torn down inside of myself. Keep holding on, cry through your pain, and allow that release to make space for God's grace. Even during your toughest moments, please know that you deserve all that God has in store for you! He wants nothing less than the best for you. I have faith that you, too, will receive the blessing that He has in store for you.

My positives:

Sometimes, our emotions can feel as if they are controlling everything about our lives. When faced with mixed emotions, you could possibly feel as though you are having a mental breakdown, and you very well could be. Take your time to digest what those emotions are trying to tell you. Your body will feel the aches and pains in specific areas. Each portion of your body has a story and a purpose. If you get headaches when you are stressed, maybe your body is telling you that your mindset needs to be adjusted. Think positive, and allow positive things to happen. If your eyes hurt, maybe your body wants you to seek God's Word, instead of focusing on things within the world around you. If your back hurts, maybe your body is telling you to take a step back, relax, and regain your focus. If your heart hurts, maybe your body is telling you to do the last thing that made your heart happy. When you feed your soul what it deserves, you will have a better vision of what God has placed right in front of you. Seek Him and receive His blessings that you have worked so hard for. It doesn't matter what others can or cannot see, only God can see the very best in you, because He is the One that created you. He knows what you are capable of and what He has equipped you with. God will forever believe in that person and that person is you. I pray that you will grow the seed that He has planted inside of you and be the person He knows you to be. Keep holding on, because your change is coming.

Now that I look back at the big picture, I realize that God favored me when He allowed me to see those flashes of life, mom's new life. In order for me to push through these difficult moments as He would have me to do, God had to allow me to release my emotions a little at a time prior to mom's transition. He has a plan and a purpose, and we must be okay with not being okay. Our brokenness has a process. Stay the course, because you were created with a purpose. You must walk through it in order to get to it. Again, God does have a plan for our lives, but we must participate in the plan for it to come to pass.

In order to help us remain on track, He will put us in situations and provide spiritual gifts to surface and give us what we need, even if we feel that we are not prepared to receive it.

I have no regrets of mine and mom's relationship. I was there when she needed me. She was there when I needed her. We have tons of wonderful memories/photos. I knew she loved me, and she knew I loved her. My siblings and father had their own personal relationship with her. My children, nieces, and nephews knew their grandmother and had a wonderful relationship with her. People around mom loved her and have nothing but sweet memories to share. Mom was one amazing woman and fulfilled her purpose of life here on Earth, and we must do the same, so her work will not be in vain.

Prayer:

Our Dear Heavenly Father, we come to you this morning to say thank you! We thank you for the love and support that surrounds us. We thank you for the strength to ask for help when needed. We thank you for the struggles that we have or will have and will overcome. We thank you for the broken bondage that is coming our way. Together, we can, and together, we will do all that we can to carry out the plans that You have for us. May we realize that our breakthrough may be for someone else that will cross our path. We claim in Your name that when that time comes, we will be solely equipped to carry out our next mission to break the chains off of someone else. We pray to always seek the positives in all situations. Allow us to be thankful and grateful for the tough moments, because that is a sign that it's our turn…our turn to do Your will. Thank You for thinking of us in a way that we never could. Thank You for the strong holds of friendship. May we be strong when others are weak. Thank You for allowing us to be able to say, "Thank You" in our weakest moments. God, we thank You for every person reading this. We thank You for our upcoming journey to carry out our mission from You. In Your name, we pray… Amen.

Tell God about your day:

_____

_____

_____

_____

_____

_____

_____

_____

_____

_____

_____

_____

_____

_____

_____

_____

Seek the positive(s) from today and write them down to see your growth over time.

_____

_____

_____

_____

_____

_____

_____

_____

_____

_____

_____

_____

_____

_____

_____

_____

Your prayer for today:

_____

_____

_____

_____

_____

_____

_____

_____

_____

_____

_____

_____

_____

_____

_____

_____

CHAPTER 2

EMOTIONAL TRIGGERS

Bible Verse:

Colossians 3:15: "Let the peace of Christ rule in your hearts, since as members of one body you were called to peace. And be thankful."

Why I choose this topic:

Today, I realize that even when a part of my soul feels a sense of peace, it sometimes shares that same space with a feeling of sadness. I am at peace knowing that mom is with the Lord and no more hurt, harm, or danger will ever come her way again. My heart continues to ache in a way that I can't even express at times because I miss our bond. The one person that knew me and made me feel most comfortable being my true self. That lonesome feeling sometimes causes destruction to my happiness. With these feelings intertwining, I seek help from the Lord. I ask Him to calm my soul, so I can feel His presence and that's where my peace comes from. Even though my happiness is interrupted often, God provides the memories and calming words from my mom to help push me through another moment in my life. For that, I am so grateful. Lord, I thank You for Your grace.

Let's Talk:

As we think of our own challenges, let's always remember that others are pushing through their own personal battles as well. May we have grace and compassion for others, even during our time of need. Lord knows I need it often. Days after my mom's transition, I noticed that I would avoid going into the living room. The Christmas tree was still up with mom's gifts waiting on her to come home. Sadly, she did not physically come back to my house. That thought still hurts. There were days where I realized that I hadn't eaten because my lower back would begin to hurt. Anxiety set in because that meant I had to cross through the living room to get to the kitchen. Each time I passed that tree, tears would accompany me. Eventually, I thought that maybe if I got the gifts and unwrapped them it would help. The unwrapping of those gifts opened up a whole new level of emotions. I could barely breathe, but ripped the wrapping paper apart as fast as I could and stuffed it in a garbage bag. I sat on my bed and cried as I placed her gifts inside the nightstand beside my bedside. I wasn't sure if I would ever open that drawer again. I remained in my room, processing what just happened as the tears sporadically fell until I finally drifted off to sleep. The Christmas tree remained up and fully decorated, because each time I tried to remove the decorations; I began to cry.

Finally, the day had come where I decided that I had to remove the tree in order to push forward a little more. I made the decision to just take the tree out to my garage fully decorated. I took a deep breath and whispered, "Lord, please help me," as I proceeded to the living room. The closer I got to the tree the more my heart pounded, but I knew I had to keep going. When I reached the tree, I grabbed it with tears in my eyes and pain in my chest. I struggled getting that big tree out to the garage, but eventually, the mission I asked God to push me through was accomplished. I went to my bathroom to release the tears that had now joined me during this process. I sat on the floor for what seemed to be hours and just cried and prayed. As time passed, I noticed that I was no longer crying, but just laid on the floor in silence, noticing the calming rhythm of my breathing pattern. God had once again provided a sense of inner peace.

Throughout the week, I noticed that some days were a little less difficult to pass through the living room. I was able to clean the living room and move on to something else. However, I still couldn't remain in there and watch television, because I would look over to the loveseat, where mom always sit and/or laid, and that was too difficult. Even with the challenges, I was still making progress. I went on to clean the kitchen. As I made it around to one of the counter spaces, I saw a jar of greens that mom had canned and brought to me and lost it. The tears visited my face once more. I allowed the emotions to release yet again. God told me to place those jars in one specific cabinet. This way, I would be able to emotionally prepare myself to open that cabinet, because I would know what was behind the door or avoid it until I was emotionally stable.

As I went back into the kitchen to be obedient to what God had told me, I felt a strength that I know was given to me by Him and Him alone. I was so thankful He was not only speaking directly to me, but walking me through this. I did as He had directed me to and was able to wipe away a few tears and continue my cleaning process. I began washing dishes (my least favorite chore) with no problems. I dried the plates and put them away. Then came the coffee mugs, and as I went to put them away, mom's favorite coffee mug appeared, along with the tears. I focused on that white mug with a pink "R" on the side. I closed the cabinet and felt as if I was never going to make it through the day without breaking down with every move I made. I ended up taking my space onto the bathroom floor. God allowed me to take my time and cry this moment out. I remember saying, "God, please help me. I miss her so much. Mom, I miss you so much." He allowed me to hear mom say, "It'll be alright." A new set of emotions came over me. I felt happy that God allowed me to hear mom say what she always told me when I needed to hear it, sad that I had to hear it in a different form, blessed that God was so immediate with my help and request again. I took my time to breathe through the pain again. God allowed me to go through the process and picked me back up to do what He wanted in that moment. That peace I spoke of previously came back to me with a stronger meaning of God's love. I sat on my bed and just relaxed in silence for as long as I needed. I can't remember if I completed my next step that day or the next. However, I was determined to carry out what God told me to do. Whenever I did reenter the kitchen, I cleared out another space in that same cabinet as mom's jar of greens and placed her favorite coffee mug on another shelf behind some items. Fast forward, I can now open the cabinet and cook some of her greens and feel her presence. Her coffee mug remains hidden, but I know it's there, and I am okay with that. I may never be able to use the mug again, but one day, I will look at it again, and another day, I may shed tears, but either way, "It'll be alright."

My Positives:

There are moments when you must give yourself time to just be in the moment of whatever emotions you are experiencing and be okay with that. Try to pull yourself out of the difficult emotions for just a moment and find one positive about your situation. As it becomes a habit, you will learn to seek positives in all situations that will lead you right back to God, the One who will carry you to your next destination in your purpose. Trust in Him, because He believes in you.

God heard my cry (literally) and pushed me through.

I was able to push through a little bit further.

I got a better understanding of the actual feeling of "peace".

I realized that it is okay not to be okay, and in order to get through these emotional triggers, I had to camouflage some things.

With God's help, I found another way to cope with the unbearable pain and felt honored that He continues to help me through this.

Today, when I was able to use what I once hid, it showed progress in this journey.

I won't have to decorate my Christmas tree next year (well…. we will cross that bridge when it comes).

When I was able to cook a jar of mom's canned greens, I felt a piece of her in the kitchen cooking with me. Memories of watching her wash, cook, me sneaking a taste of the greens as they cooled, and her canning those greens flowed through my mind. This, alone, gave me the motivation to can food just like my mom.

I still can't look at her cup, but I know it's there, and the thought allows me to feel a little of her presence.

Mom's memories are all around my house, and for that, I am so thankful to have made so many wonderful memories with her in my home. This is a true definition of "God knows the plans that He has for my life." I will praise Him through all my good and difficult moments and trust in His Word.

God provided a true definition of inner peace for me during these tough moments of my emotional triggers.

Prayer:

Our Dear Jehovah Rapha (Our Healer), Oh how I thank You! You have been the support I have needed throughout this tough time in my life. I am so thankful that You not only hear my cry, but provide me with the gift to hear from You and mom. I thank You for the gift to carry out all that You are…LOVE. I thank You for those reading this and pray over their peace and healing. I know that heartache is difficult, but with You the sense of peace is possible. I speak peace over their heart, mind, body, and soul. Once these things are received, I ask that they always have the knowledge and wisdom to give You thanks. Without You, we are nothing, and with You, we are everything… everything that You have created us to be. I thank You, once again, for love, peace, understanding, and the will to push through all circumstances, even when I don't know how. May we always hear You and carry out Your Word and Work. Our pain and healing are not always for us, but for someone else we may encounter as we journey through life. May our mission (work) be of You and carried through abundantly.

"May the words of my mouth, and the meditation of my heart, be acceptable in Thy sight, Oh Lord, My Strength, and My Redeemer. Amen." ~Psalm 19:14

Tell God about your day:

_____

_____

_____

_____

_____

_____

_____

_____

_____

_____

_____

_____

_____

_____

_____

_____

Seek the positive(s) from today and write them down to see your growth over time.

_____

_____

_____

_____

_____

_____

_____

_____

_____

_____

_____

_____

_____

_____

_____

Your prayer for today:

_____

_____

_____

_____

_____

_____

_____

_____

_____

_____

_____

_____

_____

_____

CHAPTER 3

WHEN SILENCE HITS
(LONESOME)

Bible Verse:

Lamentations 3:28: Let him sit alone in silence when it is laid on him.

Why I Choose This Topic:

I am a believer that times of silence can be some of the best moments of growth. However, loneliness often accompanies my silence. When it hits unexpectedly, a gradual release of emotions flow. As tears fall, I sometimes feel exhausted afterwards. I feel that is God's way of making room for what's to come. Lord, please fill in the broken pieces of my heart and the hearts of others with your love and comfort.

Let's Talk:

I used to call and/or text Mom multiple times throughout the day. Every day after work, I would call her to see how she was doing, and she would either answer and say, "Heeeello," or "What do you want, Gail?" We'd both giggle and begin our conversation about the day. Even when I would go into a grocery store and needed company, she was my go-to person to talk with.

After her transition, my life got quiet. I would notice that I no longer had anyone to call just to talk to about randomness or to discuss what was on my mind. The silence sometimes can become so loud and overwhelming. The feeling of loneliness comes on so strong. I no longer had anyone to talk to about my day, just sit on the phone with just to be in the company of each other, get advice on how to move forward with certain situations, laugh about inside jokes, and visit when I needed a reset to a positive outlook on everything. The feeling of loneliness is so overwhelming and hurtful. I often go to my room and allow myself to sit in silence as I process that my best friend is no longer a phone call away and no one else can fill that void. This one is still difficult at times. As I look through photos, I smile through the tears one moment and lay in tears the next. I have found myself looking really close to a photo and trying to piece together that my mom is really gone to be with the Lord. Like really gone away from us. I cried thinking about how hurt my dad, siblings, children, nieces, nephews, family, and mom's friends feel. Such an amazing woman of God gone away from those that need her most.

Once I gather my emotions, God reveals that we should never put our all into any one person, because one day, He will call them home. He created mom in His image, and she was such an amazing example of His work. So why wouldn't He want such a loving soul to stop hurting physically and live in peace with Him! I must remind myself to be happy that she made it to Heaven to be with our Heavenly

Father, and that is my goal as well one day. In the meantime, my children deserve to see and feel the fullness of love and support, just as Mom blessed me with. I am very transparent and tell them when I am having a hard time due to missing Mom. I pray to handle it in a way that will help them see how to handle sadness in a healthy manner. When I get too overwhelmed, I have learned to practice self-care by taking time away from it all and staying in a hotel, taking walks, or riding in boats while enjoying nature, and anything I can think of that will bring me back to the calm, happy, giggling, and peaceful person I love to be.

My Positives:

As I lay down my burden, I feel God pick me back up with a fullness of life. Learning that it is okay to feel sorrow, but not remain in that mindset is pushing me to be better spiritually, mentally, and physically. Remember, that sadness is a part of life and is meant to be experienced. Make room for God to put your broken pieces back together again and again. It is okay to feel broken, because God does some of His best work when you have nowhere to look, but up to the hill from which cometh your help. Let God do the work in you.

During my quiet time, I find a way to release and hear Mom tell me, "It'll be alright."

I thank God for allowing Mom to continue to communicate with me, even if it is through a different form.

During this silence, I can reset and recall on all the great memories Mom and I shared.

I can hear God even more clearly through the silence.

In my silence, God allows everything and everyone around me to become still. The many thoughts circling through my mind become one focus: God's Work.

Prayer:

Dear El Roi, The God Who Sees Me, thank You for Your love and comfort during the silence. Thank You for allowing Mom's presence to fall upon me during my time of loneliness. I understand that I can hear You more clearly during these times. Please silence my sorrow, open my heart, and activate my spiritual self, so that I may hear my next mission. I pray to hear Your plan all the way through. Please help me to carry out that plan and be equipped to move forward in this life. I love You, praise You, and thank You for it all. Amen.

Tell God about your day:

_____

_____

_____

_____

_____

_____

_____

_____

_____

_____

_____

_____

_____

_____

_____

_____

Seek the positive(s) from today and write them down to see your growth over time.

_____

_____

_____

_____

_____

_____

_____

_____

_____

_____

_____

_____

_____

_____

_____

Your prayer for today:

_____

_____

_____

_____

_____

_____

_____

_____

_____

_____

_____

_____

_____

_____

_____

CHAPTER 4

DREAMS AND VISIONS...
WHY NOT ME?

Bible Verse:

Philippians 1:3: "I thank my God for every time I remember you."

Why I Choose This Topic?

Today, I realized that I needed to speak the positives over this subject to help me see the light and hopefully help others along the way.

Let's Talk:

My dad called to wish me a happy Valentine's Day. As we talked, he stated that Mom visited him again in his dream. On this night, he saw Mom with her arms open, and when he opened his eyes, she vanished, but her image was still there. He said, "I guess that was her giving me a Valentine's Day hug." I was so happy for him, because I know he needs that from her to help heal the pain that he feels and probably would have felt on this day specifically. Over the years, he has always given Mom a Valentine's Day card and gift. To see the joy on their faces over the years have shown me what love really looks and feels like. Even through their struggles, they kept God in the midst of it all and instilled that love within each one of their children. For that, I am so thankful.

Weeks had passed and I had yet to have a dream of Mom, and I really wanted to. I would look at photos before I went to sleep, prayed for Mom to come to me in a dream, and would fall asleep with a smile on my face, knowing that, that night was going to be the one where I would get to see my mom again. The next morning would come, and I would wake up, realizing that I did not dream of her, and an emptiness would fill the atmosphere. Why was I not able to dream of Mom? We were so close, so why not me? Why was I not allowed to see her, like I wanted? I was doing everything that I could to create the environment for Mom to come into my heart as I slept, but still nothing.

After allowing my emotions to flow in disappointment, I finally decided to listen to Pastor Michael Todd's sermon from Transformation Church titled, "God Still Speaks//How Does God Speak to Us?"

His sermon helped me to realize that I was making room for something that was not meant for me. That space I was holding remained empty, because I was attempting to fill that space on my own, but God had already fulfilled His Promise. I could not see that, because I had minimized what God had for me with what I wanted for my own selfishness. Once I realized that God would not give me something that belonged to someone else, as Pastor Todd stated, I was able to enjoy His fullness in me. Those dreams were not for me at that time. He had already given me my gifts that I carry with me daily. I can hear Mom's voice when I need it most. Often, when I giggle, I hear her exact tone. I seek the positives in all situations, just as she showed me throughout her daily walk with Christ. Once I tapped into those gifts, I was able to appreciate and cherish each one on a whole new level. My heart is so full to be chosen to live with these gifts, because God knows what we need to push through this thing called life without those that we love the most.

My Positives:

God will provide everything that you need, even when you don't know what those needs are. We must be careful not to allow our faith in others to overpower our faith in God. Keep in mind He is the Creator of all mankind, and they would not be who they are without Him. His people are vessels living a life that will be pleasing in His sight. The goodness you see and seek in others is of Him and Him alone.

God has helped me realize that although I want to "see" Mom so bad, what's for me will be for me, and what is for others will be for them. So, I celebrate the gifts that others hold while working hard to share mine.

I realize and respect that God provides us with what we need, instead of what we want, in all situations.

I am blessed and thankful to be able to hear Mom and Our Heavenly Father speak to me.

I can consistently hear Mom's positives and advice come through so clearly in my time of need.

Oh, how I wish I could see her even through a dream, but God has told me to cherish the many videos and photos of and with Mom that He has blessed me with. I cherish and hold each one close. I am forever grateful.

Prayer:

Our Dear Jehovah Jireh, our Provider, I thank You! You have given me the strength to find the positives and wisdom to know what is for me will be for me. I thank You for allowing Mom to give Dad the comfort that he needs during this time. Thank You for giving me a sense of peace and understanding. May I always be grateful for what I do have, instead of focusing on the things that I don't. You are a true Provider...a Provider of what I want, Provider of what I need, and a Provider of what I will have. In this, I thank You, love You, and praise You. In Your Holy name, Amen.

Tell God about your day:

_____

_____

_____

_____

_____

_____

_____

_____

_____

_____

_____

_____

_____

_____

_____

_____

Seek the positive(s) from today and write them down to see your growth over time.

_____

_____

_____

_____

_____

_____

_____

_____

_____

_____

_____

_____

_____

_____

_____

Your prayer for today:

_____

_____

_____

_____

_____

_____

_____

_____

_____

_____

_____

_____

_____

_____

CHAPTER 5

I SAW MOM'S LIGHT
(DUST: DELICATE AND UNIQUE SPIRITUAL TRANSITION)

Bible Verse:

Genesis 3:19: "…for dust you are, and to dust you will return."

Why I choose this Topic:

Today, I reflect on how omnipotent God truly is. I love how He chooses the perfect form of communication and confirmation in our time of need. God, I thank You for being the Provider for my delicate heart.

Let's Talk:

It was the morning of mom's services, and on the way, my kids and I listened to our favorite gospel songs. The closer we got to our destination, the roads became clear. We seemed to be the only vehicle on the road. All of a sudden, I looked up into the sky and saw this circular, clear, clean, bright, white light with a ring around it. It was moving slowly and steadily toward the right. It was so beautiful. I excitedly told the kids to look into the sky, but as soon as they began to look, trees covered the light. As we got past the trees, the light had disappeared. Mixed emotions immediately came over me, because I knew that was Mom transitioning into Heaven. I was so happy she showed me that she was alright, and that she had made it into Heaven. I had no doubt that she would, but that confirmation meant so much to me. I felt her presence come all over me. That was just what I needed to give me the strength and courage to try and stand before our family and friends during her services and read the poem titled, "My Time", that I mentioned at the beginning of this book.

Fast-forwarding to her visitation service: I stood beside mom and helped my dad and siblings greet our family and friends as they came up to pay their respects. It was such comfort to be in the presence of my family, my school family, and our close friends. So many loving souls in one room and online brought together by mom. I am sure she was so pleased to see all the love that was being shown to her family during the toughest moment of our lives. God definitely places the right people in our lives at the right time. People showed up in so many ways, and it was exactly what was needed during that time.

When the line to greet the family slowed down, one of my aunties came up to stand with Mom and me. We began joking about how Mom would be telling me to "quit wearing her," meaning stop bothering her, because I kept fixing her clothes and jewelry. That was something that Mom would say jokingly, and we would laugh. During the conversation with my auntie, I started telling her about the beautiful light that I saw that morning and how it floated through the sky. Before I could complete my sentence, she finished it for me.

We looked at each other and then at Mom, realizing that we had saw that same light at the same exact time that morning. We had both seen this circular light with a ring around it. She was driving as well when she saw that same light. The fact that we both saw this light (Mom's light) gave both of us chills. I am not sure why Mom chose us, but I am so happy and blessed that she did. I hope it gives my auntie as much comfort as it does me. I replay that vision over and over in my head often.

Today, I wear a silver heart necklace with mom's fingerprint and a diamond to represent her transitioning light with an added personal message on the back for completion. This necklace brings me such comfort and strength to keep pushing and know that everything is going to be alright. I often find myself rubbing my thumb over her thumb print. I feel the ridges, and if I turn my thumb just right, I can feel the smoothness in her print. I know that not one print is the same, but just for a moment, our prints match up, and it is calming. God, thank You for the calmness that You provide to my heart, mind, and soul.

My Positives:

When our loved ones transition, so do pieces of our hearts. Change can be difficult, but it is necessary for growth. To see such a bright light that was delicate to the eyes was definitely a spiritual light from Heaven. Mom was always such a sweet and caring soul, and that light was just what I needed to continue to shine mine with the world.

I got to see the most beautiful and meaningful light.

God allowed Mom to give me what I needed in the moment.

The light was so delicate and unique.

I knew in my heart that the light was confirmation of Mom's transition to be with the Lord.

That light gave me the extra strength and support that I needed to read the message she and I wrote together to include in her obituary called, "My Time".

God spoke to me through my mother's spiritual transition.

Prayer:

Dear Jehovah Shalom, The Lord of Peace, I thank You for allowing me to experience such a beautiful transition of Mom's spirit. Thank You for seeing me as the one to carry out this mission. May I use the tools that You equip me with to help others. Please give those of Your choosing the gift to hear You, regardless of the form. Allow me to hear You and be obedient to carry out Your Will to the fullest. Please help me not ask for more than I am worthy of or meant to receive. Please allow me to be thankful for all that You are, all that You provide, and all that You protect my family and me from. I love You, praise You, and thank You. In Your name, I pray, Amen.

Tell God about your day:

_____

_____

_____

_____

_____

_____

_____

_____

_____

_____

_____

_____

_____

_____

_____

Seek the positive(s) from today and write them down to see your growth over time.

_____

_____

_____

_____

_____

_____

_____

_____

_____

_____

_____

_____

_____

_____

_____

Your prayer for today:

_____

_____

_____

_____

_____

_____

_____

_____

_____

_____

_____

_____

_____

_____

_____

CHAPTER 6

INTERPRETING MEANING

Bible Verse:

Ephesians 4:29: Do not let any wholesome talk come out of your mouths, but only what is helpful for building others up according to their needs, that it may benefit those who listen.

Why I Choose This Topic:

Some people will go out of their way to try and comfort you during your weakest moments. I was faced with conversations and statements that took me a little while to process. God allowed me to interpret meanings of conversations with Bible verses.

Let's Talk:

Throughout Mom's time in the hospital and even after her transition, doctors, nurses, friends, and family have made statements that made me stop in my tracks. No one had the intention of hurting my feelings or making me feel anything other than comfort and love.

However, when you're in a broken place, your flesh will cause you to hear things differently than they are intended. Some of the things I heard concerning Mom were things like:

"If things go downhill for her…"

"If she doesn't make it…"

"Did you know she was going to die?"

"I can't say that I know what you are going through, because I still have my mother…"

"Do you think your dad will remarry?"

"Aww, you shouldn't feel that way."

I remember going into my shell of silence. I didn't want to talk about Mom or my family to anyone until I was ready to come out of this secluded shell that I created for myself. For a moment, I felt I could not handle grief nor unwanted comments. I needed my mom to help me get through these emotional feelings that I was experiencing, because I had no clue how to work through them all.

One night, during my prayer to God, I spoke to Him specifically concerning the comments and my personal feelings. As I listened for His voice, I heard Him speak over me, "I will never give you more than you can handle." I took a deep breath, cried through my obedience, and responded with a simple, "Okay." I knew He was with me and was going to bring me back out to face the world. In that moment, God began to equip me. He was allowing me to remain in my shell until I was ready to come out and face my next. God's grace truly is sufficient.

*1 Corinthians 10:13: "No temptation has overtaken you except what is common to mankind. And God is faithful; he will not let you be tempted beyond what you can bear. But when you are tempted, he will also provide a way out so that you can endure it." I will continue to put my trust in Him to carry out His will.

My Positives:

My ability to become silence has been a powerful weapon for me during difficult conversations. Because of my obedience to God, I was able to keep my focus on Him and not have to deal with uncomfortable feelings of "I wish I hadn't reacted that way. They really did mean well." I am thankful for the village of family and friends that went out of their way to let me know that they care. I will forever be grateful to everyone who surrounded my family with love. God has truly blessed me with a loving community. I pray to always listen for God's voice and guidance, even if that means I must silence my voice to hear His.

People really do care.

God equipped me with what I needed to handle these statements and questions. My power was the power of silence. If I reacted the way I felt in that moment, I could've hurt someone's feelings when they were really trying to be a support system for me.

I realize that God is using me to speak to His people.

As I read the Bible verse for this topic, I know it is speaking directly to me. I must watch my words and know that God will always provide me with what I need, even in conversations.

I was able to read this verse and put it in perspective of my current situation:

Ephesians 4:29: "Do not let any unwholesome talk come out of your mouths, but only what is helpful for building others up according to their needs, that it may benefit those who listen."

During my quiet time with God, I was able to read it as a lesson for myself, "Kim, do not let any unwholesome talk come out of your mouth, but only what is helpful for building others up according to their needs, that it may benefit those who listen." I realized that I must respond as God would have me to and not allow myself to react on instincts. I strive to be a representation of Him.

James 1:19-20: "My dear brothers and sisters, take note of this: Everyone should be quick to listen, slow to speak and slow to become angry, because human anger does not produce the righteousness that God desires."

Prayer:

Jehovah Jireh, My Provider, I thank you for this journey entry and a clearer understanding of Your word. I will take whatever blow that comes my way and pray to be able to give people the grade that You would have me to. I could never repay You for the grace that You continue to show me. However, I return the love by showing that same grace to others. I pray to always put You first and allow You to speak for me and through me while giving You all the praise. I may not always know the meaning behind someone's actions, comments, and/or questions. However, I pray that You provide me with the response that will be pleasing in Your sight. Whether it be a facial expression, gesture, calming words, or no response at all, please, Lord, let it be of You. Lord, I love You, praise You, and thank You for it all. In your name I pray, Amen.

Tell God about your day:

_____

_____

_____

_____

_____

_____

_____

_____

_____

_____

_____

_____

_____

_____

_____

_____

Seek the positive(s) from today and write them down to see your growth over time.

_____

_____

_____

_____

_____

_____

_____

_____

_____

_____

_____

_____

_____

_____

_____

_____

Your prayer for today:

_____

_____

_____

_____

_____

_____

_____

_____

_____

_____

_____

_____

_____

_____

_____

_____

CHAPTER 7

GOD PUT ME HERE

Bible Verse:

Psalm 37:4: Delight yourself in the Lord, and He will give you the desires of your heart.

Why I Choose This Topic:

Today, I was faced with God's people unknowingly doing His work for me. God revealed to me another reason to always trust in Him and the process. He showed me that my purpose in life is to be a vessel for others. As you read this chapter, you will see how those around me unknowingly served as a vessel for my soul.

Let's Talk:

COVID-19 has invaded the lives of so many in this world. Currently, the vaccine has become available for healthcare workers, teachers (K-12), first responders, and a few others. Even after praying and scheduling my appointment to receive the vaccine, I debated for weeks and rescheduled my first appointment. I felt uneasy about the newness of the vaccine. Finally, I attempted to calm my mind and spent extra time with God. I prayed and just sat still while I listened for His answer on whether I should take this Pfizer vaccine or not.

Finally, my mind calmed, and God allowed me replay mom's conversation with me prior to her transition, "My doctor wants me to take it." Mom had already told me that her doctor wanted her to get the vaccine because of her health condition and age. I was uneasy about her getting the vaccine for the same reasons and did not want her to take a chance of something happening to her due to this vaccine. She had faith in God and knew that what was meant to happen would happen, regardless of whether she took the vaccine or not. With this memory, I knew she would have gotten it, because Mom always did everything she could to take care of herself. Then, God allowed me to hear Mom say, "It'll be alright." I'll be honest, I felt a little better about going through with it, but there was still a little bit of "what ifs" lingering in my mind. I felt bad, because I knew that I should trust God and not doubt what had been revealed to me.

Let me walk you through my experience with the vaccine. Once I got to the location where the vaccines were being given, there were tents with a couple of tall patio heaters inside. The email that I received when I signed up informed people receiving the vaccine to arrive at least 10 to 15 minutes early, which I did. As I stood under the tent, at 8:40 a.m., one of the employees came out and stated that they did not open until 9:00 a.m. and would get the line moving as soon as it was time. With that being said, we stood in line about 20 minutes, and it was about 20 degrees. I felt okay, minus my toes getting so cold they began to hurt. I could not imagine how the elderly felt. Then, all of a sudden, one elderly man with an oxygen tank came and sat in one of the chairs near me. He laughed and said, "I don't want to get too close to the heater." He was so sweet. I kept looking and smiling at him. As we continued to wait, a lady brought her elderly mom in a wheelchair and also stopped near the heater. That same man moved one of the chairs, so she could get a little closer to the heat. The daughter told her to get her gloves out of her purse, so her hands would remain warm. She looked at me, and I smiled at her, and she smiled back. Even through our masks, we could communicate a friendly smile. As I looked around, I saw so many people helping the elderly cross the street, zipping up their coats, adjusting their hats, asking if they needed a wheelchair, or wanted to move closer to a heater. It reminded me how I used to take care of Mom, even when she could do things on her own and Ms. Independent let me know that she could do everything I attempted to help her with. It warmed my heart to see the love people had for others. I could not only see it, but felt it, because I've been in that same position with my own mother. It was so genuine and reminded me of the love I continue to have for Mom.

Continuing to people watch, my spirit felt a calmness, and I remember hearing God say, "You had a lot of faith in your mom, but she had faith in Me. Always remember that your mom was created in my image. The light you see in her, is the light of Me." In that very moment, I was reminded of Genesis 1:27, "So God created mankind in His own image, in the image of God He created them; male and female He created them." I remember in that very moment, praying to myself, "God, You put me here for many reasons. Thank you, Lord for using Your people to give me what I needed in this moment. Please bless them for not only loving one another, but being a part of my healing process. In Your name I am praying, Amen."

This morning was truly something beautiful. Suddenly, the cold temperatures weren't so bad. I felt a sense of comfort and warmth from the inside out. As I entered the building, got checked in, and sat next to the nurse, I prayed over the nurse, vaccine, and the health of everyone (with and without the vaccine) and released all doubt and fear. Again, God showed me that He is still in control and will never leave nor forsake me.

My Positives:

There are moments when God will remind you of His love and promises. When He reveals Himself to you, seek the big picture. I received the confirmation that He would always be with me through it all. These confirmations went beyond a vaccine as a reminder to put my faith in Him and only Him. The goodness I saw and continue to see through Mom is God. She kept the faith in Him and all that He is, and I must do the same.

I realize that when God is speaking and we are not in a place to hear Him, He will position us to where we not only hear Him but see Him as well.

I noticed that God gave me a better understanding of how important it is to complete this devotional…the writing is for my healing, and His Words are for others as well.

I was able to see and feel God's work and messages immediately.

This is a mirror representation of the verse that speaks of how "God first loved us." Many of our parents or guardians first loved us when we were young children, so when we get the opportunity to return the favor, we cannot take that responsibility lightly.

Prayer:

Dear Jehovah Shammah (The Lord is There), I thank You for filling me with Your presence today. The way You show up is overwhelmingly breathtaking. I thank You for Your children that care deeply for their loved ones and those in need. I thank You for allowing them to be a vessel for others, even when they don't realize it. Please allow us to always be thankful for our times together. Thank You for continuing to put me through the healing process and giving me the knowledge that my strength and healing all comes from You. I pray for anyone in need of hearing, feeling, and/or seeing You in ways that are necessary for them to take just one more step into Your purpose for their lives. Regardless of where we currently are, God I know that you have so much more that is greater than we could ever imagine. Please heal us from the inside out. Make us your vessels for ourselves and others, so that we may all be united in Heaven. In Your holy and honorable name, I pray. Amen.

Tell God about your day:

_____

_____

_____

_____

_____

_____

_____

_____

_____

_____

_____

_____

_____

_____

_____

Seek the positive(s) from today and write them down to see your growth over time.

_____

_____

_____

_____

_____

_____

_____

_____

_____

_____

_____

_____

_____

_____

Your prayer for today:

_____

_____

_____

_____

_____

_____

_____

_____

_____

_____

_____

_____

_____

_____

_____

_____

CHAPTER 8

I WAS BLINDED

Bible Verse:

Isaiah 26:3: "You will guard him and keep him in perfect and constant peace whose mind [both its inclination and its character] is stayed on You, because he commits himself to You, leans on You, and hopes confidently in You."

Why I choose this Topic:

Today, I gained a better understanding of the importance of being in the presence of God without distractions.

Let's Talk:

I found a company that was able to turn the flower petals from my mom's services into a bracelet for my daughter and me, as well as a pendent for my son. I ordered them, and once our items arrived, I took one look, and they were breathtaking. I immediately tried mine on and noticed the ring of the toggle clasp made it easy for the bracelets to come undone and fall off my wrist. I told my daughter not to wear hers to school until I could find a way to fix it, because I didn't want her to lose it. A week passed, and I decided to wear my bracelet to school, but made it intentional to keep a watch on it. Throughout the day, I continued to touch my bracelet and make sure it was still secure, and it had been.

In the middle of the day, I ran into a situation where I was not a good representation of the Lord. I allowed my sassy mouth to speak in a manner that was not pleasing to Him, and I felt it in the moment I spoke. However, that did not stop me from saying what my flesh wanted to say. Nor did it stop me from sharing my feelings with a couple of others. So, not only did I disobey God by continuing to speak when I should have been quiet and kept my thoughts to myself, but poured my negativity into others. I felt the Holy Spirit convicting me from the inside out. I regretted it for the rest of the day, but the damage had already been done.

On my way home, I listened to my gospel music and got lost in my thoughts. About ten miles away from my house, I looked down at my wrist and my beautiful, custom bracelet was gone! My heart sank, and immediately, I knew God was about to teach me a lesson in obedience. I couldn't cry, because I was so numb. I knew that I could get another bracelet made, but something about that particular bracelet meant so much to me. All my focus was now on my disobedience and finding that bracelet. I wanted to call Mom so bad and talk to her about everything, but realized that was no longer an option, and if it were, I would not have gotten the bracelet in the first place. My thoughts were all over the place, and emotions were triggered once again. As soon as I pulled into my driveway, I tried to send an email to the entire staff, asking if anyone found my bracelet to please let me know, but my message would not send. I tried three times, and it would not go through. I felt myself getting so frustrated and upset, but finally, it sent. I went into the house and just sat on my bed in silence. I could not think of anything else. I was blinded by hurt and disappointment in my actions that day. Oh, the loneliness I felt from not having Mom to talk to.

When the kids got off the bus, I took them to get something for dinner because my mind couldn't focus on anything other than the loss of my bracelet. After returning home, I returned to my room. I repented and prayed all night over how I was not a good representation of God and promised to try and do much better the next day, as well as days to come. I would make a conscious effort to be better than I was the day before. I cried and prayed and prayed and cried sporadically throughout the night. Finally, I just laid on my bed, listening to instrumental meditation music, and a calmness came over me. I heard Mom say, "It'll be alright. Just calm down, leave it for a while; you'll find it." She always told me this when I would lose something. I had faith that I would find my bracelet, but there was still a tiny little "What if I don't…" lingering. That "What if" wasn't strong enough to confine me to doubts.

Eventually, I fell asleep and woke up extremely early the next morning. The bracelet was still on my mind. It's hard to explain, but I felt so emotionally exhausted, but spiritually stronger. I got ready and headed out the door. Days before, it had snowed over the ice that covered our driveway. However, the snow and ice had almost completely melted away. As I turned the corner to get into my vehicle, I was stunned and just froze where I stood! My vehicle had slid down my driveway onto the sidewalk. It was less than an inch away from being in the street. The only day that did not have a lot of snow and ice left in my driveway and my vehicle had slid. I am not sure how long I stood there blinking and dumbfounded, but I finally got myself together and walked to my vehicle, unlocked it, got inside, released my emergency break, and drove off. I thought to myself, *I am not sure whose Ring doorbell got that on camera, but I would have loved to see that, along with my facial expression as I turned that corner and saw my Jeep hanging out at the end of my driveway. Lord, if You were about to punish me for my actions, I hear and see You.* I was able to find humor in my sliding vehicle as I listened to my usual gospel stations on the way to work.

As I arrived to work, I realized that it was extremely early and immediately noticed that I was the second person to arrive. I walked straight to my classroom, and as soon as I opened my door, I looked directly at my bracelet on the floor. It was like it was waiting on me. I smiled and replayed mom's words in my head, "It'll be alright. You'll find it." Then, I heard her say one of her famous lines, "See there, I told you, you'd find it." A weight was lifted, and I was no longer blinded by one or two thoughts. It was like the gate was reopened, but with a clearer focus. Thank You, God. I know that was God telling me to keep my focus on Him and behave in a way that would always be pleasing in His sight. With that being said, I knew that my next step was to go back and correct my wrongdoings from yesterday by apologizing for my actions, which I did. It was uncomfortable, but so was the cross that was carried for me. There's a lesson in all situations. Find your positives and keep pushing forward.

My Positives:

Do you remember the story about Peter and how he denied the Lord in Luke 22? I spoke out with my flesh and not the spirit of the Lord. Neither of us were a good representation of Him and were blinded, but in different ways. Once we repented and walked in a manner pleasing to Him, we were able to see again with a clearer focus. Who are you representing on your journey with God? Know that when you mess up, you, too, can redeem yourself by taking time to be in the presence of God. He will guide you to a better place that not only He will be pleased with, but you will feel peace from the inside out. You have a purpose, and in order to get to it, He will take you through it. Continue to hang on; there is better in this world for you. There is always a lesson in your daily walk. Sometimes, when there are bigger and greater things ahead for you, God will find ways to push you into your next blessing, even if it hurts. Use that pain to push forward. You'll be faced with something greater sooner than you think. I pray God reveals Himself to you in a way that is undenying. With God, ALL things are possible, even when you feel like you have nothing left. Don't give up or give in, because you can and will get through it.

I lived through the saying, "You have to go through something to get to what God wants for you."

I spent a significant amount of time in the presence of the Lord and wanted nothing more than to feel His presence.

I could feel the comfort of my mom.

I know she is proud of my efforts in being a better person.

I know that I can't quit. I must push to be better and represent God as He would have me to do.

Prayer:

God, where do I begin, but by saying thank You! I love how you reveal things to me, even when I am not always sure what they mean in the moment. I realized that my actions had to have consequences, and thankfully, I have learned from them. I apologize for my actions and not being a great representation of Your love and compassion for others. I understand that many of us on Earth are going through our own journey with You and will act in a manner that I may not approve of, but who am I to judge! I acted in a manner that You did not approve of. I must allow people to be who they are, because that is who You created them to be. I am not perfect, nor are all my feelings. Thank You for reiterating that where I not only realize it mentally, but spiritually and physically. Please allow me to present myself as a living sacrifice by allowing You to go before me. Lord, I love You, praise You, and thank You for every lesson and blessing that comes my way. In Your name I pray, Amen.

Tell God about your day:

_____

_____

_____

_____

_____

_____

_____

_____

_____

_____

_____

_____

_____

_____

_____

_____

Seek the positive(s) from today and write them down to see your growth over time.

_____

_____

_____

_____

_____

_____

_____

_____

_____

_____

_____

_____

_____

_____

_____

Your prayer for today:

_____

_____

_____

_____

_____

_____

_____

_____

_____

_____

_____

_____

_____

_____

_____

CHAPTER 9

I FELT HIS PAIN

Bible Verse:

1 Timothy 2:1-4: First of all, then, I urge that supplications, prayers, intercessions, and thanksgivings be made for all people, for kings and all who are in high positions, that we may lead a peaceful and quiet life, godly and dignified in every way. This is good, and it is pleasing in the sight of God our Savior, who desires all people to be saved and to come to the knowledge of the truth.

Why I choose this Topic:

There have been times when I have felt the pain of others and prayed to God to serve as an intercessor on their behalf. Other times, I feel God asking me to fast without knowing my why in the moment. Through my obedience, God always reveals my purpose. As my dad came up for a visit, he spoke of Mom, and I could feel his pain so strongly. That pain inside of my dad triggered the pain inside of me.

Let's Talk:

My dad came up for his routine two-week visit (just as he and mom used to do). During his stay, I felt and saw his pain of losing mom. He even said, "I miss that woman. Many Sundays, I would make it home before her. I would wait for her to come home from church and walk down the hallway." I couldn't respond for the fear of breaking down, but I felt his pain so strongly. I missed her just as much. During his stay, we had a few laughs, but the calmness of inner emotions floated throughout the atmosphere. I was hurting for him and hurting personally. I missed seeing her curling up on my loveseat with her housecoat and blanket. I missed her laughing at me after turning on one lamp when she would say, "Turn on some light in here." I missed her riding with me to the stores to look around and laugh about nonsense." I…just…missed…her!

I had a couple of photos of mom and dad that were printed, framed, and placed on the table where Dad ate and read his Bible. I would catch him staring at their photos, and I could see a combination of his pain and love for Mom. God spoke to me, "You have interceded for so many others, but not one time have you interceded for your own father." That stopped my emotions long enough to realize what God was trying to show me during Dad's visit. My earthly father needed me, and I took that responsibility very serious. I interceded on his behalf and never told him, but I know he felt God at work. That night, I remained in the living room and slept on the couch as he slept in his chair. I needed to ask the Lord to allow me to take on some of his pain, so he could feel a sense of peace. I remained in the presence of both of my fathers holding onto the faith that God was doing a work in my dad and me. I love how God loves all of us and how I can see through my own pain to feel His love shining through to those that I love.

My Positives:

As a child, I watched Dad fast and kneel by his bedside to pray consistently. I would ask Mom about these actions, and she would take the time to explain what Dad was doing for the Lord. She explained what fasting meant and the actions that Dad was taking to be obedient during his fast. I was informed that people fast for many different reasons, but the main reason was to build upon their relationship with the Lord. I used to try the fast and never lasted a day. At an early age, I was able to learn about fasting and sacrificing things for a closer relationship with God, even when I was unsuccessful.

I realize that I must pray for Dad as much as I pray for others.

In the past, I have asked God to allow me to intercede on their behalf, and this showed that my dad needs me just as much. I will intercede on his behalf when God shows that he is in need.

God allowed me to see and feel that my dad needed me.

I must try to push through my own pain to support others when I am mentally and spiritually capable.

Prayer:

Dear Lord, I can't thank You enough for choosing me to be a vessel for others. I thank You for allowing me to not only see, but feel my father's pain. I ask that you continue to allow me to intercede on his behalf in a healthy manner (mentally, spiritually, emotionally, and physically). Please allow me to take away the pain that is unhealthy for his soul and not part of his healing process. Thank You for protecting my dad in this difficult time and allowing me to help him find comfort. May the pain that he feels be placed upon me to intercede on his behalf. Bring about peace amongst my entire family and keep us close to You and each other. May I always be able to seek You first before interceding on behalf of someone else, so that my work will be pleasing in Your sight. God, I thank You for this journey. Please cover me through every intercession that I take on in Your name. I thank You for giving me the will and strength to push through these journal entries so that they may be a blessing and part of someone else's healing process. Whatever they may face, I pray that they are able to seek Your face and find peace in midst of their storm. Lord, I thank You...I thank You, thank You, thank You for it all. In Your name I pray, Amen.

Tell God about your day:

_____

_____

_____

_____

_____

_____

_____

_____

_____

_____

_____

_____

_____

_____

_____

Seek the positive(s) from today and write them down to see your growth over time.

_____

_____

_____

_____

_____

_____

_____

_____

_____

_____

_____

_____

_____

_____

Your prayer for today:

_____

_____

_____

_____

_____

_____

_____

_____

_____

_____

_____

_____

_____

_____

CHAPTER 10

JUST FOR A MOMENT, MEDICINE WASN'T GOOD FOR MY SOUL

Bible Verses:

Psalm 147:3: "He heals the brokenhearted, binding up their injuries."

Why I Choose This Topic:

I recognize the strength that God is giving me every step of the way. I love reminiscing on wonderful memories that Mom and I have shared over the years. It can sometimes be both healing to my soul and hurtful to my heart. In both cases, God always shows up to provide the comfort that I need. They say that time heals, and I am sure it does. There are just so many broken pieces of me, but I trust God to create something in me that I have never seen before.

Let's Talk:

One morning, I decided to begin my routine cleaning of the refrigerator before grocery shopping. I threw away things, wiped down the shelves, organized items, and made room for the new. As I began to organize the condiments on the door, I saw Mom's extra medicine bottles that she kept at my house. I suddenly froze and stared at the bottle. There it was: another trigger that I didn't see coming. I closed the refrigerator in disbelief that I hadn't found it before that very moment. Lord knows that I have opened that door so many times grabbing snacks, things to cook, or a bottle of water. Suddenly, I found myself bending over, my hands grasping my knees for support, and struggling to catch my breath.

When I think back on this moment, I picture the scene in the Bible where the woman could not stand up straight until God laid His hands upon her. Although our circumstances were different, God's power remains the same. When I caught my breath, I straightened up and felt the presence of the One interceding on my behalf. I knew it was God, because my pain suddenly subsided. God, I thank You! ~Luke 13:11-13: "and a woman was there who had been crippled by a spirit for eighteen years. She was bent over and could not straighten up at all. 12 When Jesus saw her, He called her forward and said to her, "Woman, you are set free from your infirmity." 13 Then, He put his hands on her, and immediately, she straightened up and praised God. ~Hebrews 7:25: "Therefore, He is able to save completely those who come to God through Him, because He always lives to intercede for them."

My sadness did not last as long as it normally did, and I felt God's presence so strongly. He reminded me of how I was one of many who had always been there for Mom when she needed me. I remembered how Mom really needed this specific medicine, but it would cost her over $1,000 per month. None of us could afford that, and she needed it immediately. I went into action and filled out the Bausch Patient Assistance application to ask for her medicine to be covered completely. After working with a very supportive Medication Access Coordinator at the University of Louisville Hospital, within the week, Mom was approved and began receiving her medicine for free. God had showed up once again, and we were all so grateful.

God revealed these things to remind me that the way I wanted to take care of Mom without receiving anything in return is how He wanted me to do for others. There was never a hesitation in my giving with Mom. I would do anything for her without her having to ask. I loved doing things for her, because I know she would never ask, but appreciated the smallest things. I got to know Mom's wants and needs just be being in her presence and continuing to show up. If anyone would ask Mom if she wanted something, I could tell by her response if she really wanted it or not. Mom was the type who would go without to avoid "bothering" anyone. Even the simplest things, such as asking for one of her favorite desserts from McDonald's. I'd get the kids something to eat and ask her if she wanted an apple pie. If she responded, "No, I don't think I want any today," that meant she really didn't want a pie. However, if she would say, "Just get whatever the kids want," or "It doesn't matter," that meant that she wanted an apple pie, but didn't want to be any trouble. So, I would swing by McDonald's and get her a couple of pies to eat right then and a couple for later. She seriously had to be one of the sweetest people I have ever met. God, I thank you for her and our special times.

My Positives:

God knows each one of His children along with our wants and needs. That is how He is always able to supply our every need. He wants us to build relationships with each other by loving and caring for one another as He consistently does for us. Giving and doing for others and seeing their happiness brings me such joy. These are reasons that I make a great effort to practice selfcare. I can't be empty on the inside and effectively pour into others.

I feel so loved that God not only is interceding on my behalf, but I notice and feel His love in a whole new way.

When you live in a manner than represents Him, you will receive different forms of blessings in an abundance.

I have the fuel that I need to keep pushing onto the next level that God has for me.

Sadness doesn't last always. God provides stability to the life that he has created just for you.

I'm learning to position myself so I can mentally receive the happiness that God has for me.

Once I step into the life God has created for me, I will feel and be able to share my light with so many others.

I received a reminder that God knows me better than I know myself.

God wants me to know Him as well as I knew Mom and help others in the same manner, I helped her…without hesitation.

Prayer:

Dear Lord, I thank You for interceding on my behalf. I feel so honored that You are allowing me to seek Your presence throughout this journey of life. I pray that anyone who is going through a time of grief be blessed by You. May one of Your servants intercede on their behalf. May they find comfort in knowing that You are with them always. Through the tears, may we remember that it is a form of release, regardless of how long or how often it lasts. Your love is medicine for our souls, and I love You, praise You, and thank You for it all. In Your name, I pray, Amen.

Tell God about your day:

_____

_____

_____

_____

_____

_____

_____

_____

_____

_____

_____

_____

_____

Seek the positive(s) from today and write them down to see your growth over time.

_____

_____

_____

_____

_____

_____

_____

_____

_____

_____

_____

_____

_____

_____

_____

Your prayer for today:

_____

_____

_____

_____

_____

_____

_____

_____

_____

_____

_____

_____

_____

_____

_____

_____

CHAPTER 11

GOD'S WILL HURT ME

Bible Verse:

Proverbs 19:21: Many are the plans in a man's heart, but it is the Lord's purpose that prevails.

Why I Choose This Topic:

There are times when vulnerability is necessary. Holding back emotions is like telling your body it is not okay to feel this way. When our body lacks nutrients, it finds ways to tell us what is needed. Our emotions are no different. Allow the emotions to run through and out of your body to make room for what God has in store for you.

Let's Talk:

As mom laid in the hospital, I called daily to get updates on her progress and relayed the message to my siblings, family, and friends. Many times, it was difficult to hear what the nurses and doctors had to say about her status. I would take time to process all the information received and found a way to communicate it with everyone. Without realizing it, sometimes, the nurses or doctors would say things in a way my fragile heart couldn't take at the time. I dared not to relay that news in that same manner to our loved ones. I would take time to type up what they said and soften the message, so everyone would get the same information, but not as brutal. I knew they did not mean or even realize that their approach was tough for my heart to take.

In the past, I had always talked with Mom's doctors and nurses about her Sarcoidosis condition, symptoms, and more. Afterwards, I would tell her everything that was going on and our next steps. I could not wait to tell mom how much "stuff" she went through and came out on top yet again. I imagined she and I would go back through my Facebook messages on our family page and read about her battle. This is something that we always did in the past and why would this time be any different...but it was.

The one day I was allowed to go visit with Mom, I left not realizing that it would be the last time I would talk with her. I only wished she was able to open her eyes and respond on that day, but I understand that God's Will was done, and it continues to hurt. I wasn't given the chance to sit with Mom and talk about everything that she went through, how people prayed for her, what the doctors and nurses were saying while she was asleep, and how I painted a table when I would begin to feel sadness and alone while waiting for her to return home and celebrate Christmas with our family. This thought may always bring about pain in my heart and wishful thinking. I understand it was God's Will, but my flesh sometimes becomes weak, and I must listen to the memory of Mom's voice tell me, "It'll be alright," and I know she is right. God will heal the hole in my heart and fill it with His comfort and love. God will never abandon us, even during our darkest moments in life. I will continue to tell myself to keep holding on; it'll be alright.

I am thankful for the last moment that Mom and I shared. Being in her presence was a wonderful feeling mixed with a saddened heart because her state of living at the time wasn't as pleasant as I had hoped for her. I used to tell her that when she left this earth, that I would be going with her, due to a broken heart. She would tell me that I had to stay, because I had things to do. We both were right. When she transitioned, a big piece of me went with her, but the rest remains here, on Earth, to do the work of God. I do realize that I have things to do, and I will do everything I can to accomplish every journey that He places me on. I will take a piece of Mom with me as well; she will always have a piece of me, as I will her.

My Positives:

During this message, I can see how wonderful God's love truly is. Although I am saddened that I don't have my mom down here, on Earth, God came in, just like a good parent would, and removed His child from any more pain and suffering. He loves her more than we ever could. To imagine how much I love my mom and to have The One love her even more brings me peace. My mom deserves all the love that continues to surround her. My healing process comes from knowing that He gives all of us the opportunity to be alive with Him when we leave this earth. He tells us this in Romans 6:11, "*In the same way, count yourselves dead to din but alive to God in Christ Jesus.*" As we meditate on His Word, I pray that we can all overcome any obstacle that may cause doubt to what He shows us to be true.

Mom and I were able to listen to a song by CeCe Winans called "Never Lost" before her transition. She never opened her eyes during my visit with her, but I know she was listening with me.

Mom never lost her battle, because in the end, she won the ultimate prize to be with our Lord and Savior.

I know Mom heard, "Well done, My good and faithful servant."

I understand how Mom felt when she lost my grandmother, and now, she is in her presence once again.

Prayer:

Lord, I thank You for the outlook that You provide during my toughest moments. As I write this book, You continue to show my purpose in this life, and I ask that You give me the vision to see things clearly and proceed in that same manner. Allow me to put You ahead of all else and make a lasting impact on those around me. Please help with the comprehension on your Word and promises. Place Your goodness on all our hearts, minds, bodies, and souls. Regardless of what we have or currently experiencing, may we know that You are the One who can push us to be greater than we could ever imagine. God, please allow those who need support to have the courage and vulnerability to ask for it. Those who are strong in their faith and responsibilities, please allow each person to seek out to help our brothers and sisters in need, even when it doesn't look as though they need support, help us the feel the pain inside of them. Lord, please help each of us to be a fence around each other and seek the way to Your kingdom. I love You, praise You, and thank You for your goodness. In your name I pray, Amen.

Tell God about your day:

_____

_____

_____

_____

_____

_____

_____

_____

_____

_____

_____

_____

_____

_____

_____

_____

_____

Seek the positive(s) from today and write them down to see your growth over time.

_____

_____

_____

_____

_____

_____

_____

_____

_____

_____

_____

_____

_____

_____

_____

_____

Your prayer for today:

_____

_____

_____

_____

_____

_____

_____

_____

_____

_____

_____

_____

_____

_____

_____

CHAPTER 12

MOM CAME BACK TO SEE ME

Bible Verse:

Philippians 4: 6-7: "Don't worry about anything; instead, pray about everything. Tell God what you need and thank Him for all He has done. Then, you will experience God's peace, which exceeds anything we can understand. His peace will guard your hearts and minds as you live in Christ Jesus."

Why I Choose This Topic:

For days, I have been asking God to please allow me to dream about Mom, so I can see her again. Throughout my prayer time, I began to realize that what is for me will be for me. If hearing from and seeing Mom in a dream was not a part of healing, then it would not happen. I hear and feel her sweet and positive spirit in my day-to-day walk with Christ, often. Once I became content with that and trusted God to be the Provider of my comfort, I received my wish of seeing my mom in a dream.

Let's Talk:

Last night, I dreamt that Mom was allowed to come back to see me. Just for a moment, I felt complete once again, but knew it wasn't everlasting. It was like we both knew she was only visiting for a moment and would have to return to Heaven. Because of this, I don't remember us being able to speak to each other or celebrate being together. I do remember it felt nice to just be in her presence. I remember looking at her as much as I could, because I knew she would return to my memories soon. We never got close enough to hug each other, and for some reason, that wasn't an issue for either of us. I woke up and remembered her sweet spirit and presence.

God, I thank you for sharing Mom with me one more time. I miss her so much, and I can't put it into words. I wasn't prepared for that dream to happen and wanted a redo. I didn't get to ask her any questions that I would have if I was alert and prepared for her visit. I don't remember every part of the dream, but the fact that she came to me…I'm grateful. I prayed over this dream and listened for God's voice. I heard, "Be careful what you ask for, because you just may get it. It is not always in the form of our wants, but our needs. You will not always be prepared for the presentation of the delivery process., but you must always trust God's timing." Remember, what is for you will be for you and what you do with God's gifts prepares you for your next level in His mission for your life and others. Keep your eye on God and allow Him to direct your path, even when it requires you to do it alone or afraid.

My Positives:

I realize that God will provide your needs when you least expect it. There are reasons you are not given the opportunity to prepare for what's to come. If I was prepared for this dream, I may have done something to interrupt the message that was being delivered. I feel that sometimes, being still is key to a successful outcome. Remaining in the presence of Mom gave me a sense of peace and comfort. I must remember to love Him and want to seek His face just as much as I did Mom's. God's messages are so clear, but not always immediate. It took me months to realize the meaning of this dream, but the fullness of it has been a steppingstone to my next step in the journey He has for me and my family.

I got to see Mom again.

Although we both knew she had to return to Heaven, being in her presence was so nice in that moment.

I can't remember specific details, but I remember how beautiful she was in her white dress and white hat.

God continues to speak to me. He has used Mom, which always gains my attention. This is a healing process that will help me to intentionally seek Him in my daily life.

Prayer:

Dear Heavenly Father, I come to say thanks. Thank You for always listening to me and allowing me to have one of my wants met. Seeing Mom and being in her presence left me questioning what that dream meant. In reality, I should have just been thankful to You for honoring my request. I hear You and pray to always seek you in all situations, including my dreams. Please allow me to be thankful for what I have and not want more. Please allow me to always be grateful for everything that You provide in all moments. I ask that You help me to stand still, until You say move, and I seek Your guidance when it's my time to move. I pray to always put You first when figuring out my next steps to level up in Your word and work. Lord, I love You, praise You, and thank You for it all. Amen.

Tell God about your day:

_____

_____

_____

_____

_____

_____

_____

_____

_____

_____

_____

_____

_____

_____

_____

_____

Seek the positive(s) from today and write them down to see your growth over time.

_____

_____

_____

_____

_____

_____

_____

_____

_____

_____

_____

_____

_____

_____

_____

_____

Your prayer for today:

_____

_____

_____

_____

_____

_____

_____

_____

_____

_____

_____

_____

_____

_____

_____

_____

_____

_____

CHAPTER 13

MY LONELIEST MOMENTS

Bible Verse:

Matthew 11:28-30: "Come to me, all who labor and are heavy-laden, and I will give you rest. Take my yoke upon you, and learn from me, for I am gentle and lowly in heart, and you will find rest for your souls. For my yoke is easy, and my burden is light."

Why I Choose This Topic:

There are times when the emptiness can hit really hard. I'm learning that pushing through the pain sometimes requires the broken pieces of my heart to fall where they may. There is no right or wrong way to "get through", but God will lead you through during those very moments. You must learn that vulnerability is necessary and to be okay with not being okay. This may just be part of the process to your next breakthrough.

Let's Talk:

I've always heard about "the year of firsts" being difficult, but never could relate until I had no choice. From the first days without my mom, the first month, the first drive home from work without being able to call and speak with her, the first church service, the first spring break with no random Mom and me trips, the first holidays, first birthdays, first graduations, the first visit to my hometown without being able to see her face, the first time planting a garden without seeing her in it barefoot, the first cup of coffee every other weekend without her, first soccer trips without her…just all the firsts. Those moments that I once felt was so special and significant has now become memories and a part of my preparation for healing the hole in my heart.

Often, when I am driving, I begin thinking that in that moment, I would be talking to Mom on the phone telling her about my day. Since that is no longer an option, I will either listen to calming music, a sermon, or nothing at all. When I get home and settled, I feel so lonely, because Mom was my best friend, and I told her everything, even things that I'm sure she could care less about. I realized that she was my everything and I didn't care about being a part of any other group but ours. Now that she is gone, I feel so alone at times. I'll go into the feeling of not wanting anyone to try and fill that void, because that isn't possible. Then, I hear the Lord telling me to look to Him, and He will fill every void that I feel.

When reading my Bible and studying His Word, I read things that I want to share with Mom, as I did before. I have mixed emotions, because I am sad that we can't discuss the Bible and life, in general, but happy that I am still able to ask God for the determination to continue my study alone. As time goes on and while God has His hands on me, I feel that Mom is smiling, because I understand the verses that I am reading and am really proud that I am putting God first, even through my pain, in order to do right by my children, as she did for me. I made a promise to try and keep pushing to be better each day. I won't promise that sadness will not creep in and throw me off track from time to time, but I will keep going. I pray to be a vessel for my children, just as mom has always been for me.

My Positives:

During this stage of my life, I am learning to be more intentional when seeking the Lord. When I am most vulnerable, He reveals another part of my soul that I hadn't tapped into. I am grateful that He never gives up on me, even when I feel empty and struggle to pray.

I am thankful for so many memories with Mom that I can hold onto during my lonely moments.

I am learning to find a balance of wanting to be alone and seeking God when I need comfort from the hurtful silence.

I am learning to be more intentional with my prayer life and walk with Christ.

Prayer:

Lord, I pray to give You my all in every situation. Please allow me to seek You first and only move when You say to move and go where You would have me to go. Allow me to release all things that hinder my focus on You and Your promises. During my quiet time, may I hear You loud and clear and remain obedient to the purpose you have equipped with me with before I was formed in my mother's womb. I pray that I use my gifts to be a service to my fellow brothers and sisters. Allow my heart to remain pure and consistent when loving others as You first loved us. Those in need of a breakthrough from the pain and suffering, please provide them with Your undeniable peace and love. Help us to fight through our struggles of loneliness and fill us up with strength and power. Lord, release the fogginess that comes upon us during our dark moments and create a pathway for clarity and a passion to do Your will. God, I love You, praise You, and thank You for every emotion and lesson that comes with it. In Your name I pray, Amen.

Tell God about your day:

_____

_____

_____

_____

_____

_____

_____

_____

_____

_____

_____

_____

_____

_____

_____

Seek the positive(s) from today and write them down to see your growth over time.

_____

_____

_____

_____

_____

_____

_____

_____

_____

_____

_____

_____

_____

_____

Your prayer for today:

_____

_____

_____

_____

_____

_____

_____

_____

_____

_____

_____

_____

_____

_____

_____

CONCLUSION

CLAIM YOUR MIND AND
HEAL YOUR SPIRIT

As I bring this book to a close, I hope as you have read something that could support you on your spiritual journey. I am surviving and continuing to push through many rough moments in my life. This book brought out many emotions, but I pushed through to complete a purpose that God laid on my heart.

During the process of writing this book, I had completed everything except a few minor touches. One night, my laptop updated, and my entire book had been deleted, except for the rough draft. I was devastated and cried, because it had taken me months to get through it. The thought of having to relive those emotions all over again was so hurtful. I remember thinking, "I'm not doing this again." I knew that was not the attitude to take, but I wanted to be that upset in the moment, and that was okay. I could hear Mom telling me, "Just calm down you'll get it back." I took a couple of days to just walk away from it completely. I opened my document that usually automatically saves, but it hadn't this time. I tried to browse the version history, but that option was grayed out. The only option was to begin again. God will remove things from your life that is not a representation of Him and see if you will be obedient and begin again. Maybe I had written something that was not presented in a way that would represent Him, but instead distract someone from the purpose He has for them. We must continue to do His work and not allow any distractions or interruptions to overpower the Power of God's Word. He is worthy to be praised at all times. Just as He speaks to us in different forms, I pray that this book serves as a form of God's Promise to someone in need.

Also, throughout this process, I noticed that the number seven had become very significant for me. My first thought was, "How awesome is this!" Mom was the seventh out of 13 children, and she was definitely a sign of completion. She was the complete package for so many others. Studying the meaning of completion, I began to see things developing within my own life. For example, after my seventh year of teaching at one amazing school, God told me to move. Believe me, I struggled with the idea of moving from such a warm and inviting school family, but I knew that I had to be obedient and transition to my next. I cried and cried, because I loved my school, staff, and families so much. Because of this, I had a very difficult time with the transition. Please know when God speaks, you must make intentional moves. I hadn't even applied for another job position, but was called. After lots of prayers, I heard Him speak in multiple ways, telling me to go, because He had something for me at this other school.

As I was typing this paragraph, I was listening to Bishop T.D. Jakes, and he literally said, "Seven is the number of completeness." God was, without a doubt, working on me. I became so overwhelmed with His greatness. I committed to moving to the new school, because maybe someone else needed me or maybe I needed them. I knew better than to be selfish with God's love, so I made a commitment to the Lord to do as He had called me to do. I will strive to do my best to remain obedient and trust in the Lord. Just as Jeremiah 29:11 says, "For I know the plans I have for you," declares the Lord, "plans to prosper you and not to harm you, plans to give you hope and a future." Lord, I hear, trust, and will obey your every word. We hide so much in our hearts, and God knows all. He awaits us to call upon Him for strength, wisdom, and courage to make it through. We have to release the emotions and reject the negativity. I have so many doors to open and steps to take. I will do what God has for me, even if I must break. I'm not sure what's next, but I am here for the journey of God.

As you use this book and study God's Word, I pray that you find scriptures that speak to your heart and situation. I have found that making notes of scriptures can be helpful during situations that you may face. Your notes may one day serve as reminders for what God has done in your life during your time of growth. Writing out your prayers will be heart-warming when God shows up and fulfills those requests you speak into the atmosphere. Looking back at your prayers, you will see that God not only heard you, but answered your every call. We must learn to trust His timing while continuing to give Him our all until we have nothing left to give. It doesn't matter how long it takes to put yourself back together. Be proud of your process and progress. You can and will do this. May the Lord refuel your soul and give you the feeling of completion throughout your journey of claiming your mind and healing of your spirit.

Lord, I share my final prayer of this book with all that will read it. May they speak this over their own lives, and may they have a successful journey by living according to the plans that You have for them:

"Heavenly Father, I am asking that You help me to walk the way You would have me to walk, love how You would have me to love, speak the way You would have me speak, think how You would have me think, feel how You would have me feel, see the things that You would have me see, LOVE the way You would have me love, and PRAISE and GIVE THANKS to You in all that I do and all that I am in a way you would have me do so. Please help me to recognize my strengths and abilities, so that I may continue to be the vessel that You have created me to be. I thank You for being the light that shines on me and through me during the tough times and most precious moments of my life. Please help me to keep my **Faith Through Tears**. *God, I love You, praise You, and thank You for all that I have and the things that I don't. In Your holy and wonderful name, I will always pray, Amen."*

"Now may the Lord of peace Himself give you peace at all times and in every way. The Lord be with all of you."
~2 Thessalonians 3:16.

DOCUMENTARY OF MOM'S FIGHT

As mom remained in the hospital, I called multiple times a day to check on her. Due to the hospital's COVID-19 policy, she was only allowed one visitor during her entire stay, which meant that one family member would be able to see her and deliver the news to the rest of the family. This was a hard pill to swallow, because every time she was in the hospital or feeling bad, I would always to travel to be with her. I looked at the situation as at least someone could visit with her, and she would not be alone during her hospital stay. We were able to speak with her every now and then, but most days, she was so tired or could not hold the phone, due to being so weak. With each update, I would relay the message to my family. Those messages are documented here:

December 11, 2020:

Hey Family. Sorry for the long post, but our little family wanted to keep everyone informed.

Mom was experiencing some pains, so Dad and Justin took her to the ER in Campbellsville last night. Since she has that liver disease, and her liver doctor is in Louisville, they sent her there to let her doctor check her out more thoroughly. So, a bed came open around 1:00 a.m., so they took her on early this morning. She's doing well and resting.

Information from her nurse:

They have a one-visitor policy (meaning whoever goes first is the ONLY person that can go while she is there). The nurse told Dad that he could come, and he seemed so excited. We are too.

Now for the details: Mom has an UTI that is being treated. She has an acute kidney injury (don't panic). This does not necessarily mean that her kidneys are failing or anything. It could be her kidneys saying, "Hey pay attention to me.... I need water." Her nurse said the doctor will have more information once she speaks to him. They are giving fluids to help her kidney issue, and it's improving. These vitals are slightly elevated: B.U.N. is 30 and the norm is 20....her Creatinine is 1.14, and the norm is 1.03. She has been a little confused, but the nurse said it could be stemming from the liver disease and UTI. Example of her being confused: She crushed up her banana and put it in her cereal with no milk. Sometimes, mom will put bananas in her cereal, but she doesn't mash them, nor does she eat her cereal without milk. The nurse noticed she needed help with her breakfast, so she stayed there. Mom's hand was shaking, so she stayed with her and supported her, then informed mom's doctor. She said that mom tried to go to the restroom by herself (sitting on the side of her bed-trying to be sneaky I'm sure...lol). She told her, "No, let me help you." They put a bed alarm on her bed, in case she tries to be Mrs. Independent again. Lol The nurse kept talking about how she keeps looking at Mom while she's asleep and thinking how beautiful she is. She said mom hadn't ordered lunch, so she was going to do it for her. I told her that she likes her Strawberry Ensure and no greasy foods, so she put that on her list. Once her UTI and mental status improves, they will be sending her home, but they are watching her closely at this time. Shew...sorry so long, but I didn't wanna leave anything out. I will keep you updated as I hear news. We love you all!

December 13, 2020:

Good morning, Family!

Praise report this morning!!!

I just spoke with Mom's nurse, and she told me that Mom was doing well this morning. Her vitals are normal. She didn't eat much... she only took a couple of bites of fruit. I told them to try her Ensure. The nurse said they were already in the process of getting a straw to see if she'd drink that. They were already on top of it, which is a great sign she's being taken care of properly.

The nurse also told me that Mom didn't seem to be in any pain, unless they moved her, then she seemed uncomfortable. Her grip was steady this morning when the other nurse helped her bathe. Mom asked if she could get up and walk!!! They are going to get a physical therapist to come in and assist with this request. Thank You, Lord!!! I also asked what the progress was on her attempting to feed herself, so her nurse said they will try to get her in a chair for lunch and see how well she does.

Lastly, the doctor wants to put in a PICC (Peripherally Inserted Central Catheter) line. This is a long, thin tube that's inserted through a vein in her arm and passed through to the larger veins near her heart. This is better to use with stronger medication. They must have someone sign a consent form for her, so this will be done once dad arrives. Keep praying, family, because we are seeing God's work moving. We LOVE you all so much.

***Afternoon Update (4:44 p.m.):** Just called to check on mom and she's doing good and currently sleeping. The physical therapist came in earlier to try to help her walk, but she could only get to the side of her bed before experiencing pain, so she did not get to walk today. She also couldn't hold items for a long period of time without dropping them, but that's okay, she'll get there. Mom did drink her Ensure for breakfast this morning. She drank another for lunch and ate mashed potatoes and gravy.Vitals continue to look good. Keep praying she's pushing through.

December 14, 2020:

Update (5:14 p.m.):

I just talked to mom's nurse, and she said that she hasn't really eaten much today, but she has drunk her Ensure. She did throw some of it back up. They cleaned her up, and she is now sleeping and not in any pain.

I asked if they knew why she was having pains and why her grip is so weak. The nurse said that the doctor wanted them to give mom an enema, because she hasn't had many bowel movements, and that, along with the UTI infection, could be big contributors to her confusion and some pain. Ammonia buildup can also be a cause of her hands shaking. Her chest x-ray showed nothing concerning. Her white count was 12.2 (normal is 5 to 10) and continues to go down, which is good. The white count was high, due to the infection. Mom does have a TIP that previously placed inside of her, and I asked if they checked to make sure that that was okay and not causing her any pain. The nurse said yes, they looked at it, and everything was okay there. I also spoke with her care manager, and she informed me that once they set a date for Mom to be released, they are going to want to put her in home health for a little bit to help build up her strength. The location will be in Columbia, Campbellsville, or Elizabethtown (which dad stated that we will bring her home and care for her ourselves, following strict instructions from her doctors). However, they are not looking to release her at this time. They are just trying to get things in order for the future. She was asleep, so I will try to call back around dinner time, to see if I can just hear her voice and give you guys an update. Love you all!!!

December 15, 2020:

Good morning!

Mom's Morning Update:

The nurse that loves Mom so much is back on duty! They just switched shifts, so she looked into Mom's files and gave me the following information from last night: Mom did vomit a lot last night, so they gave her some medicine to settle her stomach, and she's resting. The PICC line procedure was done last night, and Mom had no issues with it. The nurse feels the UTI and lack of bowel movements were big contributors to her pain. Her labs: B.U.N. and Creatinine are back to normal, which means her acute kidney injury has been RESOLVED! It only took about 24 hours to reverse, so as a result the kidney injury was more than likely due to dehydration. That's all the information I have for now, but I will update you as I receive it. Keep those strong and specific prayers going. We love you all so much.

*Keep pushing through, Mom.

December 15, 2020:

Mom's Update (4:00 p.m.):

Mom has slept most of the day, due to some of the medications that they gave her for nausea. They have decreased those two medications, so she can be a little bit more alert. It takes a little while for the medicine to get out of her system, so once it does, her nurse said that she would let me know if she was more alert. Since she is sleeping so much, they had to put a tube through her nose and give her medicine/feed her that way, so she did not lose any of her nutrients. The nurse said that it was the easiest one she had ever put in for anybody. Later, Mom told her, "I'm going to pull this out..." (sounds just like her... she can't stand things in her nose). The nurse laughed and told her, "No you are not." She said Mom did leave it in there and didn't bother it. Lol

They did a CT scan just to rule out a stroke, and it came back NEGATIVE!

Her blood sugar was a little low this morning... it was 65, and the normal is 70. They gave her the liquid to drink, and her sugar went back up. She has not thrown up at all today, and she is currently resting. I will give another report in the morning. Love you all.

December 16, 2020:

Good morning!!! (4:30 a.m.)

I spoke with Mom's nurse, and she said that Mom has not thrown up anymore, and her vitals look good. She is breathing just fine, with the normal room air and no need for oxygen support.

They are just trying to get her ammonia levels down at this time. She said that mom still shows some signs of confusion. Mom will tell her, her name if asked, but that's about it. She did say that Mom asked for her coat and clothes. I told her she's either cold or just ready to go.... maybe both. Lol

Love that little woman. That's it for now, but I'll message everyone later: Love you all!!!

****

Dear Heavenly Father,

We come to you to say thank You. Thank You for every person reading this message and the prayers coming from their mouths and hearts. We thank You for giving Mom the strength to keep pushing. We thank You for all progress that she's made so far. We thank You for such a strong husband that will drop everything to care for Your child as You would have him to. We thank you for the doctors and nurses that are surrounding her and treating her with the knowledge and integrity that You've equipped them with. We thank You for the tears of release. We thank You for what we have and what we don't. We thank you for such a strong, God-fearing family that comes together not only in tough times, but great times. We thank You for allowing us ALL to see another day in the world You created. We thank You for the changing, renewing, and transforming parts of our lives. In Your name we pray, Amen.

December 16, 2020:

Mom's Update (3:50 p.m.):

I just spoke with Mom's nurse. She said that Mom has been a little restless today (no worries...keep reading). She would stay awake for an hour-and-a-half, and that seemed to have worn her out, so then, she would fall back asleep. However, that is progress, compared to yesterday, because yesterday, she slept the majority of her day. That sweet woman finally fell asleep about 15 minutes ago and is resting well. Nurse said that Mom was talking a little bit more. She was also more alert today vs. yesterday (eyes looking at her when she spoke)! Her vitals still look good AND the doctors are PLEASED WITH WHAT THEY SEE!!! I felt a calmness come over me this morning and prayed for more progress, as you all have. She continues to push through this, and we are so thankful!!! God is so good! We LOVE you all and the Richardson crew. Thank you so much for the love and prayers you're putting into the atmosphere.

December 17, 2020:

Good morning, family!

Mom's Update (6:30 a.m.):

I just talked to Mom's nurse. She said they moved her closer to the nurses' station because of her confusion. They can see her from there. Now for the good stuff--> She said that Mom is doing A LOT BETTER!!! She doesn't always answer their questions, but she does know that she's in the hospital majority of the time. She started Mom off with ice chips, and she did great with that, so they tried water. She's also drinking water by mouth. This morning, she was able to take her pills by mouth as well! She said that she has seen a huge and positive change in Mom. She said that Mom has been sitting up most of the night and has showed more moments of clarity. She said that Mom could hold items in her hand now, her vitals are still looking good, and they are continuing to give her the lactulose to help with her bowel movements, which are going well. The nurse said that she asked Mom if she had any kids, and she quickly told her yes and named them off, but her nurse said that she didn't know if it was our actual names or she was just naming people (because the nurse didn't know our names). I'm just gonna say I'm sure Mom called us by name. Lol She did tell me that Mom looked around and asked, "Where's Willie?" When she asked Mom, "Who's that?" Mom responded, "My husband." I know that's right, Mom. Get your husband back in there. Lol A great report this morning...thank You God. We see Your work in progress. Love you family.

Mom called Dad, Joe, so we don't know if the nurse was referring to him by what she called him, or if mom really said Willie. Either way, she knows who her husband is and wanted him with her.

December 17, 2020:

Good afternoon!

Mom's Update (4:20 p.m.):

I am a little late posting, because our little crew has been celebrating Mom's progress for today. I talked to her nurse, and she said that Mom had another good day. She is okay and still a little confused, but getting better. They continue to treat her UTI and have given her Lactulose, which will help with her elevated ammonia level. It is currently 73 today (the normal is 15 to 45). Dad said that she looked really good today and was really alert while he was there, so he was very happy about that. I got a chance to speak to her this afternoon and recorded her for the siblings. I was telling her to say hi to Dee Dee, Marc, and Justin, so she did. Then, I asked her if she knew who she was talking to. She responded, "Uhh uhh" (yes). I asked, "Who is it?" She says, "Dee Dee." I said, "This is Kim, Momma." She responded, "I know this is Kim." She's still trying to show out while she's in there. I told the siblings she better stop playing before I grab my mask and head to Louisville. Love, love that little woman. I told her everyone was praying for her. Oh, and she was able to hold the phone "independently" during our quick conversation!!! With God, her strength is miraculous!!! Again, thank you for all prayers and love. We feel it and LOVE you all so, so much.

December 18, 2020:

Good morning!

Mom's Update (6:00 a.m.):

I spoke with mom's nurse, Collin, this morning, and he said that she had another good and quiet night. She did pull out her feeding tube again, but she did very well with allowing him to put it back in. She still experiences some confusion, but she's more consistent with knowing that she is in the hospital. Her sugar was a little low, so they gave her some Ensure, and it went back to normal. She has not had much of an appetite, which is the purpose of the feeding tube...it's there to feed her the nutrients she misses when she doesn't eat her meals. This will help her vitals to remain steady. She has been able to drink Ensure, water, and take her pills by mouth with no issues. She is on a low sodium diet, so she can actually eat the food if she wanted, but she has not had much of an appetite. He said this is normal when patients experience confusion. She had one large bowel movement at midnight and another bowel movement prior to that, which is great, because it helps to get her ammonia level down. Sounds like she continues to make progress, and I hope to know more this afternoon. Love you all!!!

December 18, 2020:

Mom's Update (6:50 p.m.):

Sorry for the late update. I had to wait for her nurse to finish her rounds. She said that Mom is doing better today! Mom's more alert and experiencing less confusion than the last time she worked with her. Mom was able to answer ALL her questions, such as her name, birthday, month, year, and where she's at. Yay!!! She still does not have much of an appetite, but she is receiving the nutrients she needs. Her bowel movements have been consistent. Overall, she said that she was happy with the progress Mom is making and thinks what the doctors are doing seems to be working. I asked if she was watching TV now and she said that she was, so I told her the TV shows she enjoys. That's it for tonight. Love y'all!

December 19, 2020:

Mom's Update (1:00 p.m.):

The siblings and I just got off the phone with Mom!!! She sounds so much better. We laughed and joked about breaking Mom out of the hospital. Marcus and Justin gonna make a distraction. De Anna gonna be like Madea and drive the getaway car with Mom inside (have the cops chasing them). I'm stopping by the bank to get bail money for the crew. Mom laughed and said, "I'll be ready." She did say she had been drinking her Ensure, watching *Family Matters*, and wanted her pjs (she loves her pajamas). We had a really good call and told her you all were praying for her. She's continuing to push.

*Oh, I got too excited and forgot one important and exciting detail...SHE WALKED TODAY!!!

December 20, 2020:

Mom's Update (2:50 p.m.):

Dad is currently with Mom. We got to do another conference call with her. We had some more laughs, and she talked about how she was nibbling on some ice. During our conversation, she said, "He ate all the ice up." Dad said, "I didn't eat your ice. It's right here." Lol. She was all about her little ice chips today. I told her when she got home I was going to make her a strawberry delight, and she said, "Ohh Yeah!" After a few minutes, she said, "I'm through talking. I want to eat my ice."

I spoke with her nurse, and she said that Mom's blood pressure was low this morning, so the doctor went to visit with her ordered IV fluids. Afterwards, she became more alert and talking. She was too weak to walk earlier, but the nurse said if she felt up to it later, she would assist her. I'll keep posting as I get updates. She continues to do well with God's help and your prayers. We thank you and LOVE you all!

December 21, 2020:

Good morning!

Mom's Update (10:30 a.m.):

I just talked to mom's nurse. She said that mom's blood pressure dropped again, so the doctor came up to see her and ordered medicine for her IV. Then, it went back up. Her white count was 14 yesterday and 19 this morning (normal is up to 10) and her potassium went up, so they ordered meds for that as well. They did put her on oxygen as a precaution. I asked that they put in an order to check her ammonia level, but they had just done that and waiting for the results to come back...good job doctors and nurses. The doctor requested that she go to ICU, so they can watch her closer, because those ICU nurses only have two patients versus the seven patients the nurses have on her previous floor. Nurse Regina was happy that Mom went to ICU, because she couldn't stay with Mom as much as she wanted. I love her, and Mom does, too. She said that last night, Mom had asked if she was leaving. She told her yes, but she'd be back this morning. Then, Mom was like, "Awww...alright." Regina said that the ICU nurse will get to see Mom much more and would take good care of her. I also checked to make sure that dad could still visit Mom, and he can!!!

Lastly, she said that Mom was currently resting. I'll keep you posted once I speak with her ICU nurse.

December 21, 2020:

Mom's Update (3:20 p.m.):

Mom is currently receiving oxygen to avoid stress on her body. They are also doing CRRT dialysis. CRRT is a slower type of dialysis that puts less stress on the heart. CRRT will slowly and continuously clean out waste products and fluid from her body. By doing all these things, they should be able to finally pinpoint what and where the infection is and the overall cause of this...Yay. The move to ICU was a great one. Please keep your strong and specific prayers going. We LOVE every one of you so much.

December 22, 2020:

Mom's Update and Good News!!! (2:50 p.m.)

I talked to Mom's nurse, and he said that Mom continues to receive oxygen, but her breathing has improved 60 percent!

They have her heavily sedated, so they can get her vitals back to normal on a more consistent basis and avoid stress on her body. Once she is more stable, they will start decreasing the sedation. As the sedation decreases, she will begin to wake up slowly. At that time, they will recheck her mental status and take additional measures of getting her better. I'm so proud of that little woman. She is the strongest and toughest fighter I know.

December 24, 2020:

Hey family. There aren't a lot of details to report today, but Mom is continuing to do well, so that's a blessing. I will have more details tomorrow, and will update as soon as I do. Have a Merry Christmas, everyone. Love you all.

December 25, 2020:

Mom's Christmas Update(2:30 p.m.):

I just spoke with Mom's nurse, and he said that Mom is continuing to make progress. Her vitals are good, and they were able to take her off of the IV medication. Overnight, her heart rate dropped a little low, but it is normal now. She is receiving a medication called Midodrine, which serves as a support for her blood pressure. She has been taken off the CRRT dialysis, which continuously worked the medicine through her body 24 hours a day. Now, she is going to be put on Hemodialysis, which means she is strong enough to handle this type of dialysis...it works through her body at a faster pace. They will begin this process in the morning.

When the doctor was visiting, Mom opened her eyes, but she didn't look at him. Once she starts opening her eyes and squeezing their hands (constantly) when asked, they will then remove the oxygen tube. At that time, they will conduct what is call a Spontaneous Breathing Trial. This is where they will slowly remove the oxygen until she is breathing independently (without any support). Her current independent oxygen level is at 65 percent, which is a five percent increase since the last report.

Dad is with her now. They are going to try to see if she will open her eyes when she hears a familiar voice. Overall, Mom is pushing through and trying to get back home to us all

December 26, 2020:

Mom's Update (4:30 p.m.):

I just spoke with Mom's nurse. She said that Mom is doing about the same. Earlier, her blood pressure was a little high, and her heart rate was a little low, so they gave her some medicine in her IV, and she's doing better, so they're letting her rest. Her tube feeding went from 10 mL an hour to 20 mL an hour, which is a good thing. She opens her eyes when they talk to her, and she realizes that they are in the room. She does not squeeze their hands when asked just yet, but they are continuing to work on that. Lastly, they did not start the Hemodialysis today, but plan to do so tomorrow. Overall, she is doing well.

December 27, 2020:

Sorry I'm late posting.

Mom's Update (1:40 p.m.):

I talked to Mom's nurse, and he said that her blood pressure has been normal, heart rate is still in the 60s, and she is continuing to open her eyes. They are going to do a CT scan of her head, to make sure everything is going okay, and they will also do that hemodialysis sometime today. He did not have a timeline of when either of those things would happen, but the plan was for them to start it today.

Dad said when he went to see her, she was asleep. When he spoke to her, she looked right at him. He said that Mom looked really good and was happy with the progress he saw.

December 28, 2020:

Mom's Update (4:00 p.m.):

I spoke with Mom's nurse, and he said that her CT scan came back with normal findings!! She does have some swelling in her brain (don't panic)! It is not enough to be dangerous...it causes some of her confusion. The swelling is due to the ammonia levels that we've talked about from the beginning. Note: when you have damage to the liver, ammonia levels increase in the body. They have a machine that will be monitoring her brain waves for the next eight to twelve hours, to make sure everything remains on track. She is moving (in the bed), but not making purposeful movements, meaning she isn't moving her hands or feet when they ask her to. She does it on her own, without following their requests. They are continuing to run tests to find the overall cause of her confusion and inability to do purposeful movements at this time. She is receiving her hemodialysis, and during this process, it requires them to replace the electrolytes, potassium, etc. as the old is removed. She is improving with her oxygen! She is now only receiving 35 percent of oxygen support (21 percent is normal)!!! The team of doctors and nurses are really monitoring her closely and sounds like they are taking great care of her.

December 30, 2020:

Mom's Update (9:30 a.m.):

I spoke with Mom's nurse this morning, and he was more informative than the nurse last night. I made sure that he put in a request for me to speak to the main doctor. He did so while I was on the phone and informed me that as soon as the doctors finished their rounds this morning, they should be calling me. So, hopefully, I'll have more specific details later.

He went on to tell me that Mom is doing well and is awake more often. She's moving, but still not making purposeful movements just yet (following their commands-ex. squeezing their hands upon request). They aren't sure of the reason behind this, but will be running more tests today to see if it is infection-based or something else. They are also planning to do an MRI to check her mental status. Lastly, she is mainly breathing on her own and her ammonia levels are finally back to normal!!!

December 31, 2020:

Good morning!

Mom's Update (11:00 a.m.):

Mom's nurse said that mom's MRI showed that she has had some "small" strokes. They aren't sure when it happened. However, I'm pretty sure that's when she couldn't move her left arm. The good news is Mom is moving both sides of her body!!! She and God had already started the recovery process before that MRI. The nurse did say that her left side is a little weaker than the right, but she is moving both sides more than before. Mom has also been breathing on her own all morning! She does still have oxygen support, but only until she wakes up a little more. Once that happens, they will remove it and check her speech, etc. They don't want to remove it too soon and have something go wrong. She said the waiting part is the most difficult, but she was doing good. I haven't spoken with the doctors yet, but had the nurse actually call in my request, instead of making a note. Hopefully, I'll have more details soon, but praising Him for what I already know... He's a healer, and mom is a fighter!!!

December 31, 2020:

Doctors' Update (3:00 p.m.):

I just spoke to mom's neurology doctor. He confirmed everything I reported earlier. Their goal now is to give her time to perk up a little more, so they can see what the stroke has caused on her mind. They are also doing a very detailed test on her heart, to make sure there are no clots. They continue to work to clear up the toxins in her body. As time goes on, they want to take the tube out of her mouth, and as she makes progress, do physical therapy to help regain her strength. He said that physical therapy is down the road (maybe a couple of days, a week, or longer), but that's the overall goal.

Next, I spoke with her other doctor. He reiterated the information I've been receiving. He informed me that they've been treating the infections as they arise. She's had infection in her blood, bladder, and lungs, which caused stress on her body, which is one reason they had sedated her...to give her more comfort (she is no longer receiving that sedation medicine). Once she starts to wake up and is able to focus a little more, they will see how the stroke has affected her and proceed from there. They continue to plan ahead, so they can be ready once she perks up. He promised to stay in contact with me as often as they possibly can from this point on. This is it for now. I have to remember that it's not about the wait, but how we wait and what we do while we are waiting. God already has this figured out, and I thank Him in advance.

January 1, 2021:

Hey Family, and Happy New Year!

Mom's Update (4:00 p.m.):

I spoke with Mom's nurse. She was really sweet. She said that Mom has been doing well today. Her temperature has been good... no fevers, she's tolerating her feedings very well, having good bowel movements, and her vitals are all good. She said that there haven't been any scares at all today. She puts drops in mom's eyes sporadically to keep them hydrated. Mom hadn't been awake at all today, until Dad walked in and talked to her. She said Mom woke up a little and went back to sleep a couple of times. I suggested to her if she woke up when she heard Dad's voice, maybe try turning on some of the TV shows she likes for a bit. She liked that idea and promised to find *Andy Griffith* or *Family Matters* for her. She doesn't leave the TV going throughout the day, due to random commercials/shows that could sound violent. She doesn't want Mom thinking she's in a dangerous environment, since she's not really alert. I really liked Megan. She is really taking good care of her today and said she'd be staying in Mom's room as much as she could to watch over her. Again, we thank you for your prayers. We love you all so much, and Mom does, too!!!

January 2, 2020:

Mom's Update (3:00 p.m.):

I just spoke with Mom's nurse, and she said that Mom is having a good day! Her vitals are good: blood pressure was a little low this morning, but she received medicine, and now, it is perfect (106/50). Mom's blood normally runs a little low on a normal day...just FYI. Her heart rate is at 90 percent, which is great! Normal heart rate is 60 to100 percent. Her oxygen level is at...100 percent!!!!!! She continues to open her eyes, but not looking at them or following commands (squeeze their hand, give a thumbs up). However, she has made progress, because from 8:00 a.m.-12:00 p.m., she started looking in the direction of the nurses in her room. Way to go, Mom!

Current procedure being done: they are about to conduct a T.E.E. (Transesophageal Echo) test. This test allows the doctors to see pictures of the heart and make sure it's okay without the ribs or lungs getting in the way. This will take about an hour. She will get a little sedation. The hemodialysis will flush the sedation out throughout this process, so it doesn't affect the current progress she is making on becoming more alert...I asked this, of course. Overall, Mom continues to fight and allow God's work to shine through.

January 3, 2020:

Hey, Family. Here's Mom's Update (3:30 p.m.):

I spoke with Mom's nurse, and she didn't have a lot to report today. She said Mom threw up last night, so they took care of that by cleaning the tube and made sure she didn't have any in her system.

She said she's looking good. She's been opening her eyes sporadically and moving her feet. She said that she really moved her feet when she heard Dad's voice. She said it was so cute.

They did not conduct the T.E.E. procedure yesterday, because the doctor had an emergency with another patient. She explained that Mom's procedure wasn't an emergency procedure, due to not having major concerns. Instead, it was a standard procedure to make sure everything is remaining on track. They plan to do it later today or tomorrow. That's it for now.

January 4, 2020:

Mom's Update (4:30 p.m.):

I spoke with Mom's nurse, and she informed me that Mom is continuing to open her eyes, which is good. She still isn't making purposeful eye contact with them too often, but she has made a little contact. Early this morning, Mom started throwing up again, which caused some issues. So, they put her back on the continuous dialysis that helps flush out the unnecessary things in her body as she receives antibiotics, blood pressure medicine (her blood pressure was low), and steroids (to help with any swelling). She is now receiving 100 percent of oxygen to help with her breathing throughout this process. The doctors are going to do a CT scan of her abdomen, to see if they can find the root cause of her vomiting. They have another team of doctors that will also be working together to help Mom. I'll keep you posted when I find out more.

January 5, 2020:

Mom's Update (4:15):

I spoke with Mom's nurse, and she said that Mom is doing okay today. She continues to receive her dialysis to help keep her insides clean. She has been more awake today, which is great! She still does not follow commands, but they continue to work on that. Yesterday, she was on two different blood pressure medicines, due to the drop in her blood pressure. Today, she is only on one of those meds, AND they have already been able to reduce the amount of that medicine. She is still receiving 100 percent of oxygen, but they were able to do some oxygen exercises today. The nurse said that the exercises did not last very long, but they will continue to do them until Mom is able to breathe on her own 100 percent. Lastly, they completed the T.E.E. procedure and... they did NOT find Endocarditis (no vegetation/infection in the heart valve), which is AMAZING news! Mom is definitely the fighter we all know her to be with the Power of God.

January 6, 2020:

Hello family!

Mom's Update (4:00 p.m.):

I spoke with Mom's nurse, and she said that Mom was doing okay today. She's been awake most of the day, and once he felt as if Mom made eye contact with her, instead of the normal gazing, but she couldn't be 100 percent sure. She was awake while Dad was there. Her vitals have been good today (no more blood pressure meds). Lastly, Mom wiggled her toes ON COMMAND!!! Another great report today!!! We thank you all for the strong prayers. Each one is reaching her, and I know she feels it. Love you for your love and support through Mom's journey that will turn into a testimony.

#GodsPowerCantBeDoubtedEvenALittleBit

#GodIsOMNIPOTENT

January 7, 2020:

Mom's Update (3:30 p.m.):

I just spoke with her nurse, and she said that Mom was doing well. She has not required any sedation, so she was awake a lot this morning, but comfortable and resting now. Earlier, when the nurse asked Mom to open her eyes, she did. Then, she asked Mom to wiggle her toes, and Mom did that, too...all on command!!! Her blood pressure dropped a little this morning, but it's back to normal, along with the rest of her vitals. Her oxygen is good as well.

Yesterday, Dad said when he was visiting, the nurse asked mom to squeeze her hand (with her right hand) and wiggle her toes, and she did!!! There isn't much more to report, but this news is AMAZING!!! I'm so proud and happy for her.

January 8, 2020:

Good afternoon family.

Mom's Update (4:40 p.m.):

I spoke with Mom's nurse. She said not a lot has changed, which is good, and Mom is maintaining. Her blood pressure has been steady, along with the rest of her vitals. She's still on the CRT (continuous dialysis). She's been a little cold, so they have a Bear Hugger (a warmer that they put under her blanket-I know she loves that), and that's helping to keep her warm and temperature normal. Also, she will withdraw her hand when they pinch her fingernails. That's a test they do to make sure she is responding properly. She continues to pass that test. Another good report, and I claim more to come in Jesus' name.

This was the last entry that I could find to my family and friends. On the 9th of January, the hospital allowed two additional guests to visit with mom. My sister and I were supposed to accompany Dad, but my sister wasn't feeling well, so she decided to be safe and remain home to protect Mom. My brothers were going to visit with Mom the next morning. Dad and I headed to the hospital and spent time with Mom. She never opened her eyes, but I know she felt my presence, because I sure felt hers. It finally felt good to hold her hand, whisper inside jokes to her, and listen to some of our favorite gospel songs together. Even though I was in her presence, I still felt a deep sadness that she wasn't awake and able to see that I finally was allowed to visit with her and not call over the phone for details about her progression. I fought so hard to hold back tears while sitting in the room, listening to her machines beep and watching her sleep. Every now and then, tears would fill my eyes and fall onto my cheeks. I just wanted so bad for my mom to get better and come home to her family. Unfortunately, that did not happen. The very next morning, we all received the most devastating news that changed our lives forever. Mom fought a good fight, but no longer had to fight anymore, because God had called her home. Even with all the progress that Mom had previously made, she was now with the Lord. We know that God's plan will always be better than our own. As we move forward with Him, our family will strive to *"Trust in the Lord with all thine heart; and lean not unto thine own understanding. In all thy ways acknowledge Him, and He shall direct thy paths." ~Proverbs 3:5-6*

ABOUT THE AUTHOR

Kimberly Richardson is a God-fearing mother of two wonderful children-her son, Tristen, and daughter, Ki'en (pronounced as Cayenne). For years, she has wanted to write a book, but never dreamed the loss of her mother would be the push to complete this vision. With her calm, quiet, and loving spirit, she strives to be a positive inspiration for others. Kimberly is a woman who consistently prays that her family is a representation of God's love, peace, comfort, and promises. She cherishes her family and close friends that God has blessed her with. Her daily walk with Christ is a representation of a person in the healing and strengthening process. Determined to do the Will of God in her daily life has brought forth lots of specific prayers and changes. Seeking the presence of God during her quiet time and while admiring His creations in nature, she continues to gain strength and knowledge to push for purpose.

God has not only blessed her with two amazing children of her own, but classrooms full of amazing children receiving special education. Kimberly holds the will, determination, and love for teaching. She knows that every child can learn and be successful, when given the opportunity. Her philosophy for teaching comes from the quote by Ignacio Estrada, "If a child can't learn the way we teach, maybe we should teach the way they learn." Just as God has given His children many accommodated opportunities to learn, it is the job as His children to be the vessel for all of mankind, regardless of their age or level of abilities. Children, too, have a purpose, and God will allow each one to shine their light in their own time.

~Colossians 3:23-24: Whatever you do, work heartily, as for the Lord and not for men, knowing that from the Lord, you will receive the inheritance as your reward. You are serving the Lord Christ.